Reading SRA Mastery

·CLASSIC EDITION·

Series Guide

Levels I–6

SRA

A Division of The McGraw·Hill Companies

Columbus, Ohio

Acknowledgments
SRA/McGraw-Hill gratefully acknowledges
the authors of the *Reading Mastery*
Classic series:

Siegfried Engelmann

Elaine C. Bruner

Susan Hanner

Jean Osborn

Steve Osborn

Leslie Zoref

SRA/McGraw-Hill

A Division of The McGraw·Hill Companies

Send all inquiries to:
SRA/McGraw-Hill
8787 Orion Place
Columbus, OH 43240-4027

Printed in the United States of America.

ISBN 0-07-569393-3

7 8 9 WEB 06

Contents

Reading Mastery—Classic Edition 1

   Classic Core Components 3

   The Classic Programs 4

   Reading Mastery Classic I

      160 Lessons for Beginning Reading in Grade K or 1 6

   Reading Mastery Classic II 12

   Reading Mastery Classic I and II, Fast Cycle 16

   Components for *Reading Mastery* Classic Levels 3–6 17

   Optional Transition between 2 and 3 18

   Reading Mastery Level 3 20

   Reading Mastery Level 4 27

   Reading Mastery Level 5 34

   Reading Mastery Level 6 37

Testing and Management 41

Teaching Techniques 43

Practice Scripts 46

Scope and Sequence 62

Placement Tests 67

Sample Lessons 83

   Level I 84

   Level II 90

   Level 3 98

   Level 4 109

   Level 5 120

   Level 6 129

Pronunciation Guide .Inside back cover

Reading Mastery—Classic Edition

Reading Mastery Classic Edition is a revision of *Reading Mastery* Rainbow Edition, which was originally published in 1969 and has undergone four revisions.

A few simple principles have guided the *Reading Mastery* program since its inception in the 1960s, and they have played a large part in its resounding success.

- Along with the teacher, the program accepts complete responsibility for teaching every student how to read.
- All instruction is direct and unambiguous; tasks and activities are specified in detail.
- Every reading skill and strategy that students need is specifically taught, applied, and reviewed.
- Students receive consistent daily practice in reading, writing, listening, and speaking.
- Assessment is continuous; errors are corrected the instant they occur.

Reading Mastery Classic is appropriate for any children who do not know how to read. It is a basic reading program, which means that it teaches all the skills that are needed for the child to learn to read and comprehend what is read. It is not a full-blown language-arts program, however.

Reading Mastery Classic presents six levels (I through 6). The sequence may begin in either K or 1. It is possible to complete the sequence in either five or six years.

Reading Mastery Plus is a parallel sequence that provides a much broader language-arts context for the reading skills, but it is designed to start in K (not 1) and it presents seven levels that cover the same material that *Reading Mastery* Classic covers in six.

Learning to Read— Levels I, II, and *Fast Cycle*

Reading Mastery Classic I, II, and *Fast Cycle* focus on learning to read. This process involves decoding, but not only decoding. To read, students must be able to both decipher the symbols and understand what they mean. Initially, children learn to decode words through a special "orthography" that goes beyond phonics by showing letters that go together to make a unique sound. The orthography shows **th, sh, ch, wh**, and **er** as joined letters that make a single sound. The orthography also shows that letters with lines over them make a long-vowel sound. The orthography also provides for small letters that are silent. The net result is that all words in the program are spelled correctly, but the long lines and joined combinations permit students to decode words (such as **were** and **where** and **wāit**) as perfectly regular words (and without ever having to learn verbal "phonics rules").

The special orthography is maintained through Level I and part of II. During this period, children learn to decode various words and engage in practice that builds greater fluency. After children have become fluent decoders, the prompted orthography is systematically replaced with details of standard orthography. This transition begins in Level II and is completed by Lesson 86.

Throughout Levels I and II, decoding is taught explicitly and systematically. Students learn sounds, words presented in isolation, and stories. All words are composed entirely of letters and combinations that students have learned. All stories are composed entirely of words that students have learned as words presented in isolation. This sequence assures that students will be successful in reading stories and will be able to focus on the meanings. They will not tend to make word-reading mistakes because the words are familiar.

The real measure of a reading program lies in its ability to teach comprehension. In *Reading Mastery*, comprehension is specifically taught—not just tested—from the very first lesson. Students in *Reading Mastery* learn how to answer questions and how to make stories come alive. They learn the meanings of words and the forms of sentences. They draw story pictures and follow written instructions. They soon learn—through these and other techniques—how to comprehend the texts they decode.

Reading to Learn— Levels 3 and 4

Reading Mastery Levels 3 and 4 focus on reading to learn. Levels 3 and 4 shift the emphasis from learning how to decode and understand what the text says and implies to using these skills as tools to learn new facts and relationships. Levels 3 and 4 have both information passages and related story sequences that teach students about different places in the world, different times—from the age of the dinosaurs to the present, different planets, different important events, and different activities. Students learn facts and rules that they apply to living near the North Pole, diving deep in the ocean, migrating with a flock of geese, traveling with a fly, and traveling through outer space and through the human body. The combination of information passages and engaging stories transforms science rules and historical facts into experiences that set the stage for content-area reading. It also provides a strong foundation of information and skill in different content areas.

Understanding Literature— Levels 5 and 6

In Levels 5 and 6, students extend what they have learned about reading stories and facts and begin to analyze and interpret literature. This transition involves learning to read new styles, new sentence forms, and new vocabulary. It also involves new comprehension skills for interpreting different types of literature. Students read classic and contemporary novels, short stories, poems, myths, folktales, biographies, and factual articles. Through daily writing activities, students compare different writers and analyze specific details of plots, characters, and themes. In addition to answering direct questions about the material they read, students complete a variety of comprehension activities that teach specific concepts and strategies. Students identify contradictions, interpret figurative language, draw inferences, and analyze the logic that characters use in making decisions. Students also interpret maps, graphs, and forms. Extended writing activities and explicit instruction in interpretation and analysis sharpen skills in understanding the perspective or viewpoint of a character, identifying motives, and identifying themes.

Classic Core Components

The tables below show the core reading components for each level, I through 6, and the optional components.

Classic Core Components

Student Materials	I	II	Fast Cycle I/II	3	4	5	6
Storybooks	♦	♦	♦				
Textbooks				♦	♦	♦	♦
Take-Home Books	♦	♦	♦				
Workbooks				♦	♦	♦	♦
Teacher Materials							
Reading Presentation Books	♦	♦	♦	♦	♦	♦	♦
Teacher's Guide	♦	♦	♦	♦	♦	♦	♦
Audiocassette	♦		♦				
Teacher's Take-Home Book and Answer Key	♦	♦	♦				
Answer Key				♦	♦	♦	♦
Spelling Book	♦	♦	♦				
Writing and Spelling Guide				♦			
Behavioral Objectives	♦	♦	♦	♦	♦	♦	♦
Skills Profile Portfolio	♦	♦	♦	♦	♦	♦	♦

Optional Components

	I	II	Fast Cycle I/II	3	4	5	6
Literature Guide and Read-to Collection	♦	♦	♦				
Literature Guide and Student Anthology				♦	♦	♦	♦
Benchmark Test Books and Handbook	♦	♦	♦				
Testing and Management Handbook						♦	♦
Independent Reader Libraries	♦	♦	♦ ♦				
Seatwork (Blackline Masters)	♦	♦	♦ ♦				
Assessment Manual	♦	♦	♦				
Language Arts Guide				♦	♦	♦	♦
Activities across the Curriculum				♦	♦	♦	♦

The Classic Programs

Classic Core Materials

For the teacher:

- *Presentation Books* (all levels)

  These books contain presentation scripts for every lesson. The scripts tell the teacher what to say and do. The scripts also specify the students' answers. Many scripts provide specific procedures for correcting the students' mistakes. In Level II through Level 6, the *Presentation Books* also contain reproductions of the student material.

- *Teacher's Guides* (all levels)

  These guides explain the programs in detail and suggest specific teaching techniques for many of the program activities. The guides also contain correction procedures, suggestions for classroom management, and other material helpful to the teacher.

- *Audiocassette* (Level I and *Fast Cycle*)

- *Behavioral Objectives* (all levels)

  A complete listing of the behavioral objectives for each skill taught in the program. In Levels 3–6, these appear in the *Teacher's Guides*.

- *Skills Profile Folders* (all levels)

  Individual portfolios that allow the teacher to keep track of each student's skill mastery. In Levels 3–6, these appear in the *Teacher's Guides*.

- *Teacher's Take-Home Book and Answer Keys* (Levels I, II, *Fast Cycle*)
  Answer Keys (Levels 3–6)

  These books contain answer keys for the student *Take-Home Books, Workbooks,* and *Textbooks*.

- *Spelling Books* (Levels I, II, *Fast Cycle*)
  Writing and Spelling Book (Level 3)

  These books contain spelling (and writing) lessons that can be presented after the other program activities are completed.

For the students:

- *Storybooks* (Levels I, II, *Fast Cycle*)
- *Textbooks* (Levels 3–6)

  These hardbound, full-color books contain the illustrated stories, novels, poems, information passages, and vocabulary words that the students read.

- *Take-Home Books* (Levels I, II, *Fast Cycle*)

  These consumable books contain questions and exercises that the students complete during each lesson. The students write the answers to *Take-Home Book* questions in the *Take-Home Book*. There is one perforated page for each lesson. After the students complete a page, the teacher checks their work. Then the students take the page home to show to their parents or guardians.

- *Workbooks* (Levels 3–6)

  These consumable books contain questions about the *Textbook* stories, as well as vocabulary and skill exercises. Students write the answers to *Workbook* questions in the *Workbook*.

Optional Materials

For Levels I and II:

- *Literature Guide* and *Read-to Collection*
- *Benchmark Test Books* and *Handbook*
- *Independent Reader Libraries*
- *Seatwork* (Blackline Masters)
- *Assessment Manual*

For Levels 3–6:

- *Literature Guide* and *Anthology*
- *Language Arts Guide*
- *Activities across the Curriculum*
- *Mastery Test Handbooks* (Levels 5 and 6)

Classic Core Activities

Every lesson in *Reading Mastery* Classic Edition consists of teacher-directed activities and independent student activities.

Teacher-Directed Activities

- *Prereading Exercises* (Levels I, II, and *Fast Cycle*)

  The students learn letter sounds and master decoding and comprehension readiness skills.

- *Word Practice* (all levels)

  The students read lists of words aloud, both in unison and individually. These words will later appear in the reading selections.

- *Vocabulary Exercises* (Levels 3–6)

  The students learn the meanings of difficult words that will later appear in the reading selections.

- *Skill Exercises* (all levels)

  The teacher explains the skill exercises contained in the students' *Take-Homes, Workbooks,* or *Textbooks.*

- *Group Reading* (all levels)

  The students take turns reading aloud from their *Storybooks* or *Textbooks.*

- **Comprehension Questions** (all levels)

  Both during and after the group reading, the teacher presents comprehension questions about the reading.

- *Individual Reading Checkouts* (Levels I–5)

  In selected lessons, the teacher measures each student's decoding rate and accuracy.

- *Workcheck* (all levels)

  The teacher checks the students' independent work.

- **Spelling** (Levels I–3)

  The teacher conducts spelling activities. In Level 3, the teacher conducts writing and spelling activities.

Independent Student Activities

- *Silent Reading* (all levels)

  The students read stories, questions, and exercises silently.

- *Story Items* (all levels)

  The students answer questions about the stories.

- *Skill Items* (all levels)

  The students complete exercises that teach specific decoding, comprehension, literary, and study skills.

- *Vocabulary Items* (Levels 3–6)

  The students use new vocabulary words to complete sentences and work crossword puzzles.

- *Review Items* (all levels)

  The students review previously taught skills and vocabulary.

- *Fact Games* (Levels 3–5)

  The students play games that involve facts they have learned.

- *Special Projects* (Levels 3–6)

  The students complete special projects that relate to their reading selections.

- *Writing Assignments* (Levels 3–6)

  The students write on assigned topics.

- *Supplementary Novels* (Levels 4–6)

  The students read novels independently and complete comprehension activities for each novel.

Reading Mastery Classic I

160 Lessons for Beginning Reading in Grade K or 1

Reading Mastery Classic Edition, Level I contains 160 daily lessons that teach basic decoding and comprehension skills. Decoding is taught through an explicit phonics method that stresses letter sounds and blending. Students practice decoding by reading word lists and stories, both aloud and silently. Comprehension activities include answering questions about pictures, following directions, and responding to a variety of questions based on the stories.

Classic Core Materials

For the teacher:

- *Presentation Books* (3)
- *Teacher's Guide*
- *Spelling Book*
- *Teacher's Take-Home Book and Answer Key*
- *Behavioral Objectives Book*
- *Skills Profile Folder*
- *Audiocassette* demonstrating how to pronounce the sounds and how to present tasks from the program.

For the students:

- *Storybooks* (3)
- *Take-Home Books* (3)

The *Storybooks* contain original stories written especially for the program. There are both realistic and fantasy stories about animals and people.

Sample Activities (first half)

In the first half of *Reading Mastery I* the students master decoding and comprehension readiness skills, learn individual letter sounds, and learn how to read regularly spelled words.

The following tasks from Lesson 34 are typical of those found in the first half of the program. Task 1 (shown below) prepares the students for decoding by teaching them how to pronounce specific sounds. First the teacher says a sound; then the students say the sound in unison. The teacher uses a simple signal to make sure the students respond together. After the group has mastered the sound, individual students say the sound.

Task 1 also prepares the students for comprehension by teaching them how to follow directions. Every task in the *Presentation Books* involves directions that the students must follow.

PRONUNCIATION

TASK 1   Children say the sounds

a. **You're going to say some sounds. When I hold up my finger, say** (pause)   **c. Get ready.** Hold up one finger. *c.*

b. **Next sound. Say** (pause)   **ĭĭĭ. Get ready.** Hold up one finger. *ĭĭĭ.*

c. **Next sound. Say** (pause)   **nnn. Get ready.** Hold up one finger. *nnn.*

d. **Repeat** *c* **for sounds** *c,* **ĭĭĭ, and nnn.**

e. **Call on different children to do** *a, b,* **or** *c.*

f. **Good saying the sounds.**

Lesson 34

Task 2 teaches the students how to read the letter **i**. The teacher holds the *Presentation Book* so that the students can see the large **i**. First the teacher touches under the **i** and says the letter's sound: ĭĭĭ. Then the students say the sound in unison as the teacher touches under the letter. The students practice saying the sound until every student has mastered it. Finally, individual students say the sound.

A new letter sound is introduced every few lessons. The students learn every lowercase letter, as well as the sound combinations **th, sh, ch, ing, er, oo, wh,** and **qu,** and the word **I.** Long and short vowels are treated as separate letters. For example, short *a* (as in *mat*) is taught in Lesson 1, and it always looks like this: **a.** Long *a* (as in *mate*) is taught in lesson 58, and it always has a macron over it: **ā.** In *Reading Mastery II,* the students learn other ways of distinguishing between long and short vowels, and the macron is no longer used.

In Task 13, the students learn how to read a regularly spelled word. First the students identify the individual letter sounds in the word. Then they sound out the word. Finally, they read the word by "saying it fast."

This simple and effective sounding-out procedure allows the students to read hundreds of regularly spelled words.

SOUNDS

TASK 2   Introducing the new sound i as in if

a. Touch the first ball of the arrow for **i. Here's a new sound. My turn to say it. Get ready.** Move quickly to the second ball. Hold. **iii.**
b. Return to the first ball. **My turn again. Get ready.** Move quickly to the second ball. Hold. **iii.**
c. Return to the first ball. **My turn again. Get ready.** Move quickly to the second ball. Hold. **iii.**
d. Return to the first ball. **Your turn. Get ready.** Move quickly to the second ball. Hold. *iii.* **Yes, iii.**
e. Return to the first ball. **Again. Get ready.** Move quickly to the second ball. Hold. *iii.* **Yes, iii.**
f. Repeat *e* until firm.
g. Call on different children to do *d.*
h. **Good saying iii.**

Lesson 34

READING VOCABULARY

TASK 13   Children say the sounds, then sound out the word

a. Touch the first ball of the arrow for **am. You're going to sound it out.** Point to the ball for **a. What sound are you going to say first? Touch the ball.** *aaa.* **Yes, aaa.** Point to the ball for **m. What sound are you going to say next? Touch the ball.** *mmm.* **Yes, mmm.**
b. Return to the first ball. **Everybody, when I move my finger, say the sounds aaammm. Don't stop between the sounds. Get ready.** Move quickly under each sound. Hold. *Aaammm.*
c. Return to the first ball. **Again. Sound it out. Get ready.** Move quickly under each sound. Hold. *Aaammm.*
d. Repeat *c* until firm.
e. Return to the first ball. **Say it fast. Slash.** *Am.*
   Yes, am. You read the word am. Do you know who I (pause) am?
f. Call on different children to do *c* and *e.*

Lesson 34

After they finish the *Presentation Book* activities, the students complete exercises in their *Take-Home Books*. The *Take-Home Book* exercises develop and expand the skills taught in the *Presentation Book*. First the teacher goes over the exercises with the students; then the students complete the exercises on their own. In the tasks shown below, the students follow pictured directions, copy letters, pair letters with objects, and complete a picture.

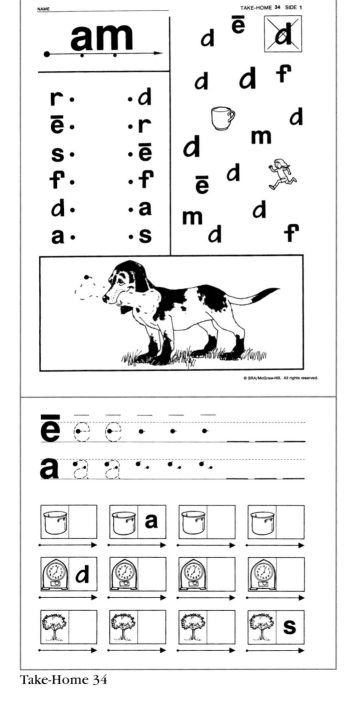

Take-Home 34

Sample Activities (second half)

In the second half of *Reading Mastery I*, the students read complete stories, answer comprehension questions, and learn how to read a number of irregular words.

The following tasks from Lessons 113 and 115 are typical of those found in the second half of the program.

By the second half of the program, the students have learned almost all the lowercase letters, as well as several sound combinations. In the task shown below, the teacher presents the sound combination **ch**. The two letters that make up this sound are connected by a heavy black line. This unique orthography is used for all sound combinations in *Reading Mastery I*. In *Reading Mastery II*, the students learn other means of recognizing sound combinations, and the letters are disjoined.

ch

SOUNDS

TASK 1   Teaching ch as in chat

a. Point to **ch**. Here's a new sound. It's a quick sound.
b. My turn. (Pause.) Touch **ch** for an instant, saying: ch. Do not say chuh.
c. Again. Touch **ch** and say: ch.
d. Point to **ch**. Your turn. When I touch it, you say it. (Pause.) Get ready. Touch **ch**. *ch.*
e. Again. Touch **ch**. *ch.*
f. Repeat *e* until firm.

Lesson 113

The students continue to learn new regularly spelled words. They also learn how to read irregular words, how to read words "the fast way," and how to read words in lists. The *Presentation Book* page below contains a typical group of tasks.

In Task 11, the students read an irregular word: **arm**. First the students sound out the word. Then the teacher tells the students how to say the word correctly. Finally, the students practice reading the word.

A new irregular word is introduced every few lessons. The program teaches more than fifty irregular words.

In Tasks 12 and 13, the students read a word that rhymes with *arm*: **farm**. Because this new word is so similar to the word presented before, the students are able to read the new word without first sounding it out.

In Task 14, students sound out and read the word **teach**. The *a* is smaller than the other letters in the word. The students have already learned the rule, "When a word has a little sound, you don't say the sound." This rule allows the students to sound out words with silent letters. In *Reading Mastery II*, the students learn other means of identifying silent letters, and all letters become the same size.

In Task 15, the students read all the words on the page "the fast way." When they read words "the fast way," the students simply read the words without sounding them out. Finally, in Task 16, individual students take turns reading the words.

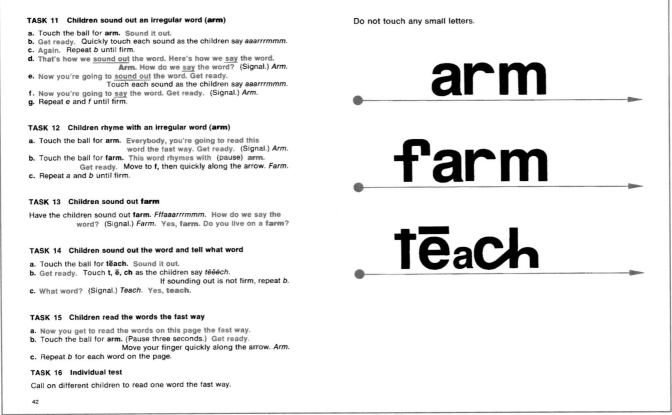

TASK 11   Children sound out an irregular word (arm)

a. Touch the ball for **arm**. Sound it out.
b. Get ready. Quickly touch each sound as the children say *aaarrrmmm*.
c. Again. Repeat *b* until firm.
d. That's how we <u>sound out</u> the word. Here's how we <u>say</u> the word.
      Arm. How do we <u>say</u> the word? (Signal.) *Arm*.
e. Now you're going to <u>sound out</u> the word. Get ready.
      Touch each sound as the children say *aaarrrmmm*.
f. Now you're going to <u>say</u> the word. Get ready. (Signal.) *Arm*.
g. Repeat *e* and *f* until firm.

TASK 12   Children rhyme with an irregular word (arm)

a. Touch the ball for **arm**. Everybody, you're going to read this
      word the fast way. Get ready. (Signal.) *Arm*.
b. Touch the ball for **farm**. This word rhymes with (pause) **arm**.
      Get ready. Move to *f*, then quickly along the arrow. *Farm*.
c. Repeat *a* and *b* until firm.

TASK 13   Children sound out farm

Have the children sound out **farm**. *Fffaaarrrmmm*. How do we say the
      word? (Signal.) *Farm*. Yes, **farm**. Do you live on a **farm**?

TASK 14   Children sound out the word and tell what word

a. Touch the ball for **tēach**. Sound it out.
b. Get ready. Touch **t, ē, ch** as the children say *tēēēch*.
      If sounding out is not firm, repeat *b*.
c. What word? (Signal.) *Teach*. Yes, **teach**.

TASK 15   Children read the words the fast way

a. Now you get to read the words on this page the fast way.
b. Touch the ball for **arm**. (Pause three seconds.) Get ready.
      Move your finger quickly along the arrow. *Arm*.
c. Repeat *b* for each word on the page.

TASK 16   Individual test

Call on different children to read one word the fast way.

42

Do not touch any small letters.

READING VOCABULARY Lesson 115

Beginning in Lesson 91, the students read entire stories in their *Storybooks*. These stories are written with words the students have already learned. Initially, the stories are only a few sentences long. By the end of the program, however, the students are reading longer stories that are serialized over a span of lessons.

The story-reading activities for Lesson 115 are shown below. In Task 21, the teacher reads the title of the story. The students learn that the title tells what the story is going to be about. In Task 22, the students read the entire story "the fast way," without sounding out any words. After they finish this first reading, the students review any words they had trouble with. Then, in Task 24, they read the story again, as the teacher asks literal and interpretive comprehension questions.

Most of the teacher's questions can be answered by specific words in the story. The students answer these questions in unison, at the teacher's signal. Some questions, however, require the students to make personal judgments or predictions. These questions are answered by individual students.

In Task 25, after the students finish the story, they predict what a picture of the story would look like. Then they turn the page and look at a picture of the story. The teacher presents comprehension questions about the picture. Later, the students will draw their own picture of the story.

The *Take-Home* for Lesson 115 has four sides. (Sides 1 and 2 are shown on the next page.) The students copy letters and sentences, match words, follow pictured directions, and associate words with pictures. They also draw a picture of the day's story in the blank space on side 2. The teacher explains all of the exercises before the students complete them.

Lesson 115 also includes an individual reading checkout and a bonus *Take-Home* (Tasks 33 and 34 shown on the next page). The checkout requires the students to read for rate and accuracy. As the group is working independently, the teacher calls on individual students to read the day's story aloud. The students earn stars if they can read the entire story in less than two minutes, while making no more than three errors.

lots of cars

a man on a farm has lots of cars. hē has ōld cars. hē has littlₑ cars.

arₑ his cars fōr gōₐts? nō.

56

arₑ his cars fōr shēēp? nō. arₑ his cars fōr cows? nō.

his cars arₑ fōr cops. hē has lots of cop cars.

57

58

TASK 21 Teacher introduces the title

a. Pass out Storybook 1.
b. Open your book to page 56.
c. Hold up your reader. Point to the title. **These words are called the title of the story. These words tell what the story is about. I'll read the title the fast way.**
d. Point to the words as you read: Lots of cars.
e. Everybody, what is this story about? (Signal.) *Lots of cars.* **Yes, lots of cars. This story is going to tell something about lots of cars.**

TASK 22 First reading—children read the story the fast way

Have the children reread any sentences containing words that give them trouble. Keep a list of these words.

a. Everybody, touch the title of the story and get ready to read the words in the title the fast way.
b. First word. Check children's responses. (Pause three seconds.) Get ready. Clap. *Lots.*
c. Next word. Check children's responses. (Pause three seconds.) Get ready. Clap. *Of.*
d. Repeat c for the word **cars.**
e. After the children have read the title, ask: What's this story about? (Signal.) *Lots of cars.* Yes, **lots of cars.**
f. Everybody, touch the first word of the <u>story</u>. Check children's responses.
g. Get ready to read this story the fast way.
h. First word. (Pause three seconds.) Get ready. Clap. *A.*
i. Next word. Check children's responses. (Pause three seconds.) Get ready. Clap. *Man.*
j. Repeat i for the remaining words in the first sentence. Pause at least three seconds between claps. The children are to identify each word without sounding it out.
k. Repeat h through j for the next two sentences. Have the children reread the first three sentences until firm.
l. The children are to read the remainder of the story the fast way, stopping at the end of each sentence.
m. After the first reading of the story, print on the board the words that the children missed more than one time. Have the children sound out each word one time and tell what word.
n. After the group's responses are firm, call on individual children to read the words.

TASK 23   Individual test

a. Look at page 56. I'm going to call on different children to read a whole sentence the fast way.
b. Call on different children to read a sentence. Do not clap for each word.

TASK 24   Second reading—children read the story the fast way and answer questions

a. You're going to read the story again the fast way and I'll ask questions.
b. Starting with the first word of the title. Check children's responses. Get ready. Clap. *Lots.*
c. Clap for each remaining word. Pause at least three seconds between claps. Pause longer before words that gave the children trouble during the first reading.
d. Ask the comprehension questions below as the children read.

After the children read:	You say:
Lots of cars.	What's this story about? (Signal.) *Lots of cars.*
A man on a farm has lots of cars.	What does he have? (Signal.) *Lots of cars.*
He has little cars.	What kind of cars does he have? (Signal.) *Old cars and little cars.*
Are his cars for goats?	What do you think? *The children respond.* Let's read and find out.
No.	Are they for goats? (Signal.) *No.*
He has lots of cop cars.	What kind of cars does he have? (Signal.) *Cop cars.*

TASK 25   Picture comprehension

a. What do you think you'll see in the picture? *The children respond.*
b. Turn the page and look at the picture.
c. Ask these questions:
   1. Do you see lots of cop cars? *Yes.*
   2. What would you do if you had all those cop cars? *The children respond.*

INDIVIDUAL CHECKOUT: STORYBOOK

TASK 33   2-minute individual checkout — whole story from title

a. As you are doing your take-home, I'll call on children one at a time to read the **whole story**. Remember, you get two stars if you read the story in less than two minutes and make no more than three errors.
b. Call on a child. Tell the child: **Start with the title and read the story carefully the fast way. Go.** Time the child. Tell the child any words the child misses. Stop the child as soon as the child makes the fourth error or exceeds the time limit.
c. If the child meets the rate-accuracy criterion, record two stars on your chart for lesson 115. Congratulate the child. Give children who do not earn two stars a chance to read the story again before the next lesson is presented.

   49 words/**2 min** = 25 wpm [**3 errors**]

TASK 34   Bonus take-home: sides 3 and 4

After the children have completed their take-home exercises, give them sides 3 and 4 of Take-Home 115. Tell them they may keep the stories and read them.

In Task 34, after the children have completed their take-home exercises, the teacher gives them sides 3 and 4 of Take-Home 115. The students read the bonus take-home story, color it, and take it home.

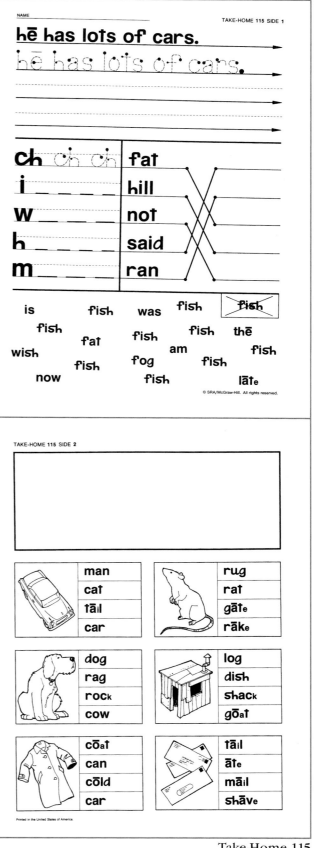

Reading Mastery Classic II

Reading Mastery Classic Edition, Level II contains 160 daily lessons that expand basic reading skills. Students in the program learn strategies for decoding difficult words and for answering interpretive comprehension questions. They also learn basic reasoning skills, such as making inferences and drawing conclusions. The daily reading selections include realistic fiction, fantasy, and factual articles.

Classic Core Materials

For the teacher:

- *Presentation Books* (3)
- *Teacher's Guide*
- *Teacher's Take-Home Book and Answer Key*
- *Spelling Book*
- *Behavioral Objectives Book*
- *Skills Profile Folder*

For the students:

- *Storybooks* (2)
- *Take-Home Books* (3)

The *Storybooks* contain original stories written especially for the program, as well as adaptations of famous children's stories. Many of the stories are serialized over a span of lessons.

Sample Activities

Each lesson in *Reading Mastery II* begins with word practice tasks. These tasks appear in the *Presentation Book*. In the first part of the program, the teacher presents individual sounds and words, and the students read them aloud. Later in the program, the teacher presents lists of words that the students read aloud.

In Lessons 1–47, the unique *Reading Mastery I* orthography is used for all words. In Lessons 48–92, the *Reading Mastery I* orthography is gradually phased out and replaced by standard orthography. During this transition period, the students learn the final-e rule and other guides for reading words in standard orthography. They also learn every capital letter. In Lessons 93–160, standard orthography is used in all the student materials.

The following activities appear in Lesson 97. The lesson begins with four separate word lists. The list in Task 1 contains new words that are difficult to decode, as well as words that the students have already learned. The new words are printed in red. The teacher first reads the new words; then the students spell them. Finally, the students read the new words. After the students have mastered the new words, they read the entire list.

The students read all of the words in unison. When the teacher points to a word, the students look over the word and get ready to read it. Then they read the word in unison as the teacher slashes under the word with a finger.

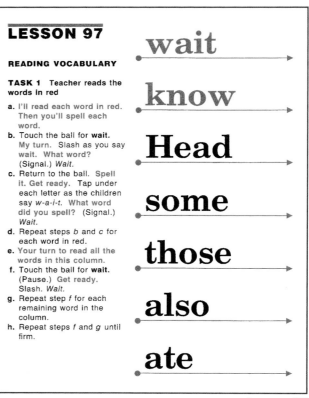

LESSON 97

READING VOCABULARY

TASK 1 Teacher reads the words in red

a. I'll read each word in red. Then you'll spell each word.
b. Touch the ball for **wait**. My turn. Slash as you say **wait**. What word? (Signal.) *Wait.*
c. Return to the ball. Spell it. Get ready. Tap under each letter as the children say *w-a-i-t*. What word did you spell? (Signal.) *Wait.*
d. Repeat steps *b* and *c* for each word in red.
e. Your turn to read all the words in this column.
f. Touch the ball for **wait**. (Pause.) Get ready. Slash. *Wait.*
g. Repeat step *f* for each remaining word in the column.
h. Repeat steps *f* and *g* until firm.

wait
know
Head
some
those
also
ate

Lesson 97

In Task 2, the students read words that contain various sound combinations, word endings, or root words. These word elements are underlined in each word. The students first read the underlined part; then they read the entire word.

These underlined-part word lists teach students an important decoding strategy. The lists demonstrate that many unfamiliar words are made up of familiar parts. By identifying these familiar parts, the students are able to decode unfamiliar words.

In Task 3, the students read new words that are easy to decode or words they have already learned. The teacher points to each word; then the students read the word when the teacher slashes under it with a finger.

In Task 4, the students spell each word before reading it. This procedure not only promotes accurate spelling, but also teaches the students to examine words carefully.

After the group finishes reading all the lists, individual students take turns reading one list each.

TASK 2 Words with underlined parts

a. First you're going to read the underlined part of each word in this column. Then you're going to read the whole word.
b. Touch the ball for **string**. Read the underlined part. Get ready. Tap the ball. *Ing.* Read the whole word. (Pause.) Get ready. Slash. *String.*
c. Repeat step *b* until firm.
d. Repeat steps *b* and *c* for each remaining word in the column.
e. Repeat the column until children read all the words in order without making a mistake.

string

stand

stones

cash

TASK 3 Read the fast way

a. You're going to read all the words in this column the fast way.
b. Touch the ball for **Let's**. (Pause.) Get ready. Slash. *Let's.*
c. Repeat step *b* until firm.
d. Repeat steps *b* and *c* for each remaining word in the column.
e. Repeat the column until the children read all the words in order without making mistakes.

Let's

who

ice cream

didn't

hopping

But

Liked

TASK 4 Children spell, then read

a. First you're going to spell each word. Then you're going to read that word the fast way.
b. Touch the ball for **hoping**. Spell it. Get ready. Tap under each letter as the children say *h-o-p-i-n-g.* Return to the ball. Read it. Get ready. Slash. *Hoping.*
c. Repeat step *b* for each remaining word in the column.
d. Repeat steps *b* and *c* until firm.

hoping

tame

bite

then

cone

right

tiger

Individual test

a. Call on different children to read one column of words from the lesson.
b. Praise children who read all words with no errors.

READING VOCABULARY Lesson 97

After the word-practice tasks are completed, the teacher directs the students as they read aloud from their *Storybooks*. During this group reading, the teacher monitors the students' decoding accuracy and also presents comprehension questions.

The students begin the group reading by reading the first part of the story within a specified decoding error limit. The first part of the story extends from the title to the circled 5. The teacher calls on individual students to read two or three sentences in turn. The students must practice reading the story until they can read up to the circled 5 while making no more than five decoding errors.

The *Presentation Book* contains reproductions of the *Storybook* pages. Numbers are placed within these reproductions to indicate where the teacher is to present comprehension questions. The actual questions are printed under the reproduced pages.

After the group reads the first part of the story within the error limit, the teacher rereads the first part and presents the comprehension questions. Then the students take turns reading the rest of the story, as the teacher presents more comprehension questions.

The comprehension questions teach a variety of literal and interpretive comprehension skills. In this sample lesson, the students relate titles to story content, answer literal questions, identify the meanings of common words, and predict narrative outcomes.

STORYBOOK

STORY 97

TASK 5 Reading—decoding

a. Pass out Storybook 2.

b. Everybody, open your reader to page 38.

c. Remember, if the group reads all the way to the red 5 without making more than five errors, we can go on.

d. Everybody, touch the title of the story. Check.

e. If you hear a mistake, raise your hand. Remember, children who do not have their place lose their turn. Call on individual children to read two or three sentences. Do not ask comprehension questions. Tally all errors.

To correct word-identification errors (**from**, for example)

1. That word is **from**. What word? *From.*

2. Go back to the beginning of the sentence and read the sentence again.

---

f. If the children make more than five errors before they reach the red 5: when they reach the 5 return to the beginning of the story and have the children reread to the 5. Do not ask comprehension questions. Repeat step *f* until firm, and then go on to step *g*.

g. When the children read to the red 5 without making more than five errors: read the story to the children from the beginning to the 5. Ask the specified comprehension questions. When you reach the 5, call on individual children to continue reading the story. Have each child read two or three sentences. Ask the specified comprehension questions.

The Tame Tiger Who Liked Ice Cream[1]

There once was a tame tiger. This tiger did not bite children.[2] He didn't eat goats or sheep.[3] He said, "I like ice cream.[4] So I will go to town and get some."

But the tiger didn't have any cash.[5] He said, "I will fill my pouch with round stones. I hope that the man at the ice cream store likes round stones."[6]

So the tiger filled his pouch with round stones. Then he walked to town. He went up to the man at the ice cream stand.

"I don't have any cash," the tiger said. "But I have a pouch filled with pretty round stones."[7]

"Let's see them," the man said.

So the tiger showed the man his stones. The man said, "I like those stones. They are pretty."[8]

The tiger gave the pouch to the man.(5)

Then the tiger said, "I want a big cone, and I want some string."[9]

The man said, "What will you do with a big cone and some string?"

"Wait and see," the tiger said.

What do you think the tiger did?[10] He ate the ice cream from the cone.[11] Then he put the big cone on his head with a string.[12]

The tiger said, "I love ice cream and I love hats. I ate the ice cream and now I have the best hat in town."[13]

The man at the ice cream stand said, "That tiger is very tame. He is also very smart."

The end

---

[1] What is this story going to be about? (Signal.) *The tame tiger who liked ice cream.* A tiger is an animal with stripes.

[2] Did this tiger bite children? (Signal.) *No.* Right. He was tame.

[3] I wonder what he did eat! Let's read some more.

[4] Now we know. What does he eat? (Signal.) *Ice cream.*

[5] What didn't he have? (Signal.) *Cash.* What's cash? *The children respond.* Right. He didn't have any money.

[6] What does the tiger want to do with the round stones? *The children respond.*

[7] Does he have cash? (Signal.) *No.* What does he have? (Signal.) *Pretty round stones.*

[8] Did the man like those stones? (Signal.) *Yes.*

[9] What did the tiger say? (Signal.) *I want a big cone, and I want some string.*

[10] What do you think? *The children respond.* Let's keep reading.

[11] What's the first thing that the tiger did? (Signal.) *He ate the ice cream.*

[12] What's the next thing he did? (Signal.) *The children respond.*

[13] How did he get that hat? *The children respond.* Right. He made it from the cone and string.

STORY Lesson 97

After the students finish reading the story, they complete written exercises in their *Take-Home Books*. In this sample lesson, the students answer questions about the story, follow written directions, and complete deductions. They also read a short passage and answer questions about the passage.

The teacher explains new exercises to the students. In this sample lesson, the teacher explains the deductions exercise. The students do the remaining exercises on their own.

DEDUCTIONS
The children will need pencils.

TASK 7 Picture deductions

a. Pass out Take-Home 97 to each child.

b. Hold up side 2 of your take-home and touch the sentence in the box in the deductions exercise.

c. Everybody, touch this sentence on your take-home. Check children's responses.

d. Call on a child. Read the sentence in the box. *All the big horses are tired.*

e. Everybody, say that rule. (Signal.) *All the big horses are tired.* Repeat until firm.

f. You know that some of the horses in the picture are tired. What kind of horses are those? (Signal.) *All the big horses.* Everybody, touch a horse you know is tired. Check.

g. You don't know about the horses that are not big. Everybody, touch a horse you don't know about. Check.

h. Call on a child. Read the instructions below the box. *Circle every horse that is tired.*

i. Everybody, what are you going to do? (Signal.) *Circle every horse that is tired.* Yes, circle every horse that you know is tired.

j. Do it. Check.

INDEPENDENT ACTIVITIES

TASK 8 Summary of independent activities

Everybody, now you'll do your take-home. Remember to do all parts of the take-home and to read all the parts carefully.

Lesson 97

NAME _____   TAKE-HOME **97**   SIDE **1**

1. The tiger was _____ .
   lame   old   tame   time

2. Did he bite children? _____

3. What did he like to eat? _____
   ice   ice bits   ice cream   ice skates

4. Did the tiger have any cash? _____

5. What was in his pouch? _____
   stops   cones   stones   rocks

6. Did the man like the stones? _____

7. Who said, "What will you do with a big cone and some string"? _____

8. Who said, "Wait and see"? _____

9. The tiger made the cone into a h_____ .

| The boy felt cold in the rain. |

1. Make a box around the word that tells how the boy felt.

2. Make a box around the words that tell where the boy is.

3. Make a line over the words that tell who felt cold.

TAKE-HOME **97**   SIDE **2**

One day, the boss left a note for Sid. Here is what that note said: "Tape my cane with a bit of white tape. The white tape is in the tape can."
Do you think Sid did what the note said? Yes, he did. After he looked at the note, he got the white tape and taped the cane.

1. Who left the note for Sid? _____

2. The note told Sid to _____ a cane.

3. Where was the white tape? _____
   in the tap can   in the tape can

4. Sid got the tape and taped the _____ .

| All the big horses are tired. |

Circle every horse that is tired.

Printed in the United States of America.

Take-Home 97

Reading Mastery Classic I and II, *Fast Cycle*

Reading Mastery Classic Edition, *Fast Cycle I and II*, is an accelerated beginning-reading program for children of average or above-average ability. *Fast Cycle* provides a one-year first-grade program of 170 daily lessons. After completing *Fast Cycle II*, the children should go into a third-level reading program (ideally *Reading Mastery* Level 3). In the third grade, they should be placed in a fourth-level program, and so forth, completing six years of reading instruction in only five years and being at least one year accelerated in skill development.

Fast Cycle includes many tasks from *Reading Mastery I and II*, but it presents the tasks on an accelerated schedule. For example, in *Reading Mastery I*, a new letter is generally introduced in every fourth lesson; in *Fast Cycle I*, a new letter is generally introduced in every second lesson. The faster rate is appropriate for above-average students.

The placement test for *Reading Mastery I* can be used to determine if students should be placed in *Fast Cycle*. The test appears on pages 67–69 of this guide.

Core Materials for *Fast Cycle*

- *Teacher's Guide*
- *Spelling Book*
- *Teacher's Take-Home Book and Answer Key*
- *Behavioral Objectives Book*
- *Skills Profile Folder*

For *Fast Cycle I* (Lessons 1–80)

- *Audiocassette* demonstrating how to pronounce the sounds and how to present tasks from the program.
- *Storybook 1*
- *Take-Home Books A* and *B*
- *Presentation Books A* and *B*

For *Fast Cycle II* (Lessons 81–170)

- *Storybook 2*
- *Take-Home Books C* and *D*
- *Presentation Books C* and *D*

Optional Materials for *Fast Cycle*

- *Fast Cycle* Assessment Manual
- *Fast Cycle* Benchmark Test Books and Handbook
- *Reading Mastery Classic I* Seatwork and *Reading Mastery Classic II* Seatwork
- *Reading Mastery Classic I* Independent Readers Libraries and *Reading Mastery Classic II* Independent Readers Libraries
- *Reading Mastery Classic II* Literature Guide and *Read-to Collection*

Fast Cycle **Lesson Correlation Chart**			
Fast Cycle I	*Reading Mastery I*	*Fast Cycle II*	*Reading Mastery II*
Lesson	Lesson	Lesson	Lesson
1	12	81	11
10	29	90	40
20	45	100	52
30	64	110	79
40	82	120	89
50	102	130	106
60	120	140	116
70	140	150	126
80	158	160	150
		170	160

Components for Reading Mastery
Classic Levels 3–6

Levels 3–6 of the *Reading Mastery* program are available in two versions: *Reading Mastery* Classic option and *Reading Mastery Plus* option. The Classic option is a reading-only program; the *Plus* option is a complete language-arts program that teaches both reading and language.

The core reading components (teacher materials, student textbooks, student workbooks) of both versions are identical. The *Plus* option, however, features several additional language-arts components—a *Literature Anthology*, a *Literature Guide*, a *Language Arts Guide*, and an *Activities across the Curriculum* project book. An option for Levels 5 and 6 is a *Reading Mastery Plus* Testing and Management system.

All language-arts components from the *Plus* option are available as separate components for *Reading Mastery* Classic users.

Classic Core Components

	3	4	5	6
Student Materials				
Textbooks	◆	◆	◆	◆
Workbook(s)	◆	◆	◆	◆
Teacher Materials				
Reading Presentation Books	◆	◆	◆	◆
Teacher's Guide	◆	◆	◆	◆
Answer Key	◆	◆	◆	◆
Writing and Spelling Guide	◆			

Optional Components

	3	4	5	6
Literature Guide and Student Anthology	◆	◆	◆	◆
Language Arts Guide	◆	◆	◆	◆
Activities across the Curriculum	◆	◆	◆	◆
Testing and Management Handbook (Mastery Tests)			◆	◆

Optional Transition between 2 and 3

Reading Mastery Plus, Level 2, Lessons 96–160

The last 65 lessons of *Reading Mastery Plus*, Level 2 may be presented after children complete *Reading Mastery* Classic, Level 2. The transition introduces word lists in the student reader (not in the teacher presentation book) and other forms of independent work that provide added preparations for Level 3.

This transition is particularly appropriate for children who complete Level 2 Classic mid-year. The transition to Lesson 96 of *Plus* is very smooth because it involves familiar skills and reading vocabulary.

Reading Mastery Plus, Level 2 Materials

For the teacher:

- *Reading Presentation Book C*
- *Teacher's Guide*
- *Answer Key*
- *Behavioral Objectives Book*
- *Skills Profile Folder*

For the students:

- *Textbook*
- *Workbook C*

Beginning in Lesson 96, *Reading Mastery Plus*, Level 2, the word lists appear in the students' Textbook. Students spell each word instead of sounding it out. *Presentation Book C* contains presentation scripts for the word lists, as well as reproductions of the student lists.

The following activities appear in Lesson 96.

Textbook

EXERCISE 1

READING WORDS

a. From now on, you're going to read everything from your textbook. Your book has the word lists you'll read and the stories you'll read.
- Open your textbook to lesson 96. Find the farmhouse. ✓
- (Teacher reference:)

> 1. ugly
> 2. motor
> 3. bay
> 4. horn
> 5. tug
> 6. mind
> 7. bragged

b. You'll spell each word and then tell me the word.
c. Spell word 1. Get ready. **(Tap 4 times.)** *U-G-L-Y.*
- What word? **(Signal.)** *Ugly.*
d. Spell word 2. Get ready. **(Tap 5 times.)** *M-O-T-O-R.*
- What word? **(Signal.)** *Motor.*
e. Spell word 3. Get ready. **(Tap 3 times.)** *B-A-Y.*
- What word? **(Signal.)** *Bay.*
f. Spell word 4. Get ready. **(Tap 4 times.)** *H-O-R-N.*
- What word? **(Signal.)** *Horn.*
g. Spell word 5. Get ready. **(Tap 3 times.)** *T-U-G.*
- What word? **(Signal.)** *Tug.*
h. Spell word 6. Get ready. **(Tap 4 times.)** *M-I-N-D.*
- What word? **(Signal.)** *Mind.*
i. Spell word 7. Get ready. **(Tap 7 times.)** *B-R-A-G-G-E-D.*
- What word? **(Signal.)** *Bragged.*
j. Let's read those words again the fast way.
- Word 1. What word? **(Signal.)** *Ugly.*
- (Repeat for remaining words: **motor, bay, horn, tug, mind, bragged.**)

Lesson 96

EXERCISE 2

READING WORDS

a. Find the fence. ✓
- (Teacher reference:)

> 1. noon
> 2. tubby
> 3. boat
> 4. contest

b. You'll spell each word and then tell me the word.

c. Spell word 1. Get ready. **(Tap 4 times.)** *N-O-O-N.*
- What word? **(Signal.)** *Noon.*

d. Spell word 2. Get ready. **(Tap 5 times.)** *T-U-B-B-Y.*
- What word? **(Signal.)** *Tubby.*

e. Spell word 3. Get ready. **(Tap 4 times.)** *B-O-A-T.*
- What word? **(Signal.)** *Boat.*

f. Spell word 4. Get ready. **(Tap 7 times.)** *C-O-N-T-E-S-T.*
- What word? **(Signal.)** *Contest.*

g. Let's read those words again the fast way.
- Word 1. What word? **(Signal.)** *Noon.*
- (Repeat for remaining words: **tubby, boat, contest.**)

EXERCISE 3

READING WORDS

a. Find the barn. ✓
- (Teacher reference:)

> 1. <u>smok</u>ing
> 2. <u>sleek</u>est
> 3. <u>smash</u>es
> 4. <u>puff</u>ed
> 5. <u>dump</u>y
> 6. <u>strong</u>er

b. Each word has a part that is underlined. You'll tell me the underlined part, then the whole word.

c. Word 1. The underlined part is **smoke.** What's the underlined part? **(Signal.)** *smoke.*
- What's the whole word? **(Signal.)** *Smoking.*

d. Word 2. What's the underlined part? **(Signal.)** *sleek.*
- What's the whole word? **(Signal.)** *Sleekest.*

e. Word 3. What's the underlined part? **(Signal.)** *smash.*
- What's the whole word? **(Signal.)** *Smashes.*

f. Word 4. What's the underlined part? **(Signal.)** *puff.*
- What's the whole word? **(Signal.)** *Puffed.*

g. Word 5. What's the underlined part? **(Signal.)** *dump.*
- What's the whole word? **(Signal.)** *Dumpy.*

h. Word 6. What's the underlined part? **(Signal.)** *strong.*
- What's the whole word? **(Signal.)** *Stronger.*

i. Let's read those words again the fast way.
- **Word 1. What word?** (Signal.) *Smoking.*
- (Repeat for remaining words: **sleekest, smashes, puffed, dumpy, stronger.**)

Reading Mastery Level 3

Reading Mastery Level 3 contains 145 daily lessons that emphasize reasoning and reference skills. Students in the program learn how to apply rules in a wide variety of contexts and how to interpret maps, graphs, and time lines. The program also introduces a number of complex sentence forms and a range of vocabulary activities. The daily reading selections include realistic fiction, fantasy, and factual articles.

Classic Core Materials

For the teacher:

- *Presentation Books* (3)
- *Teacher's Guide*
- *Answer Key*
- *Writing and Spelling Guide*

For the students:

- *Textbooks* (3)
- *Workbooks* (3)

The *Textbooks* contain stories and comprehension passages written especially for the program. Most of the stories are serialized over a span of lessons, and many of the stories incorporate science facts and rules. Here is a partial listing of the *Textbook* contents.

- **A Tricky Toad Named Goad**—A toad has amusing adventures in which she tricks people.
- **Nancy Learns About Being Small**—A girl becomes very small and learns important facts about common objects.
- **Herman Travels the World**—A fly goes around the world on a jet. The students use maps to follow the jet's progress.
- **Linda and Kathy Alone on an Island**—Two girls are shipwrecked and struggle to survive on an island.
- **Bertha and Her Nose**—A girl with a great sense of smell helps an investigator capture a group of polluters.
- **Andrew Dexter's Dreams**—A bank teller gets superhuman powers and is hired by a football team.

- **The Time Machine**—Two boys find a time machine and go back and forth in time.
- **Comprehension Passages**—Short passages that provide background information for the stories.

Sample Activities

The following vocabulary activities appear in Lesson 52 of *Reading Mastery* Level 3.

The students begin Lesson 52—and most other lessons—by working on model vocabulary sentences. These sentences contain selected vocabulary words. Students learn what each sentence means, practice saying each sentence, and respond to tasks about the meanings of specific words. In Lesson 52, exercise 1, below, a new model sentence is introduced.

VOCABULARY SENTENCES

LESSON 51 – 100

13. The smoke swirled in enormous billows.

EXERCISE 1

VOCABULARY

a. **Find page 397 in your textbook.** ✓
- Touch sentence 13. ✓
- This is a new vocabulary sentence. It says: The smoke swirled in enormous billows. Everybody, read that sentence. Get ready. (Signal.) *The smoke swirled in enormous billows.*
- Close your eyes and say the sentence. Get ready. (Signal.) *The smoke swirled in enormous billows.*
- Again. Say the sentence. Get ready. (Signal.) *The smoke swirled in enormous billows.*
- (Repeat until firm.)
b. When smoke **swirls,** it spins around as it drifts. If you mix chocolate syrup in milk, you'll see swirls of brown and white. What's a word that means **spun around?** (Signal.) *Swirled.*

---

c. Things that are **enormous** are very, very large. What's another way of saying **The building was very, very large?** (Signal.) *The building was enormous.*
d. **Billows** are large clouds or waves that are swelling up.
e. Listen to the sentence again: The smoke swirled in enormous billows.
  • Everybody, say that sentence. Get ready. (Signal.) *The smoke swirled in enormous billows.*
  • (Repeat until firm.)
f. What word means that the smoke spun around and around? (Signal.) *Swirled.*
  • What word means **very, very large?** (Signal.) *Enormous.*
  • What word tells you that the clouds were swelling up? (Signal.) *Billows.*
  • (Repeat step f until firm.)

In the next exercise of Lesson 52, students read the word lists.

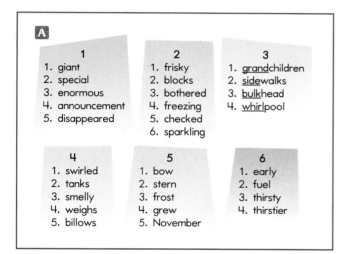

A

1	2	3
1. giant	1. frisky	1. grandchildren
2. special	2. blocks	2. sidewalks
3. enormous	3. bothered	3. bulkhead
4. announcement	4. freezing	4. whirlpool
5. disappeared	5. checked	
	6. sparkling	

4	5	6
1. swirled	1. bow	1. early
2. tanks	2. stern	2. fuel
3. smelly	3. frost	3. thirsty
4. weighs	4. grew	4. thirstier
5. billows	5. November	

There are three types of lists. The first type consists of words that are difficult to decode (such as **giant**). The teacher reads these words to the students. Then the students read the words and spell them.

READING WORDS

Column 1

a. Find lesson 52 in your textbook. ✓
  • Touch column 1. ✓
  • (Teacher reference:)

1. giant	**4. announcement**
2. special	**5. disappeared**
3. enormous	

b. Word 1 is **giant**. What word? (Signal.) *Giant.*
  • Spell **giant**. Get ready. (Tap for each letter.) *G-I-A-N-T.*
c. Word 2 is **special**. What word? (Signal.) *Special.*
  • Spell **special**. Get ready. (Tap for each letter.) *S-P-E-C-I-A-L.*
d. Word 3 is **enormous**. What word? (Signal.) *Enormous.*
  • Spell **enormous**. Get ready. (Tap for each letter.) *E-N-O-R-M-O-U-S.*
e. Word 4 is **announcement**. What word? (Signal.) *Announcement.*
f. Word 5 is **disappeared**. What word? (Signal.) *Disappeared.*
g. Let's read those words again, the fast way.
  • Word 1. What word? (Signal.) *Giant.*
  • (Repeat for words 2–5.)
h. (Repeat step g until firm.)

The second type of list consists of words that have a common feature, such as a common sound or a common ending. The teacher explains the common feature; then the students read the words.

For each word in the lists with a meaning that may not be familiar to the students (such as **frisky**), the teacher gives an explanation of the meaning.

Column 2

i. Find column 2. ✓
- (Teacher reference:)

1. frisky	4. freezing
2. blocks	5. checked
3. bothered	6. sparkling

- All these words have endings.
j. Word 1. What word? (Signal.) *Frisky.*
- **Frisky** means **playful** or **full of energy.** What's another way of saying **The cats were playful?** (Signal.) *The cats were frisky.*
k. Word 2. What word? (Signal.) *Blocks.*
  - (Repeat for words 3–6.)
l. Let's read those words again.
  - Word 1. What word? (Signal.) *Frisky.*
  - (Repeat for words 2–6.)
m. (Repeat step l until firm.)

Column 3

n. Find column 3. ✓
- (Teacher reference:)

1. <u>grand</u>children	3. <u>bulk</u>head
2. <u>side</u>walks	4. <u>whirl</u>pool

- All these words are compound words. The first part of each word is underlined.
o. Word 1. What's the underlined part? (Signal.) *grand.*
  - What's the whole word? (Signal.) *Grandchildren.*
p. Word 2. What's the underlined part? (Signal.) *side.*
  - What's the whole word? (Signal.) *Sidewalks.*
q. Word 3. What's the underlined part? (Signal.) *bulk.*
  - What's the whole word? (Signal.) *Bulkhead.*
r. Word 4. What's the underlined part? (Signal.) *whirl.*
  - What's the whole word? (Signal.) *Whirlpool.*
s. Let's read those words again.
  - Word 1. What word? (Signal.) *Grandchildren.*
  - (Repeat for words 2–4.)
t. (Repeat step s until firm.)

Column 4

u. Find column 4. ✓
- (Teacher reference:)

1. swirled	4. weighs
2. tanks	5. billows
3. smelly	

- All these words have endings.
v. Word 1. What word? (Signal.) *Swirled.*
  - (Repeat for words 2–5.)
w. Let's read those words again.
  - Word 1. What word? (Signal.) *Swirled.*
  - (Repeat for words 2–5.)
x. (Repeat step w until firm.)

Column 5

y. Find column 5. ✓
- (Teacher reference:)

1. bow	4. grew
2. stern	5. November
3. frost	

z. Word 1 rhymes with **how.** What word? (Signal.) *Bow.*
a. Word 2. What word? (Signal.) *Stern.*
- The bow is the front of a ship. The stern is the back of the ship. What do we call the front of a ship? (Signal.) *Bow.*
- What do we call the back of a ship? (Signal.) *Stern.*
b. Word 3. What word? (Signal.) *Frost.*
- Frost is frozen water that forms on grass during cold nights. When the temperature goes up in the morning, the frost disappears.
c. Word 4. What word? (Signal.) *Grew.*
- Word 5. What word? (Signal.) *November.*
d. Let's read those words again.
  - Word 1. What word? (Signal.) *Bow.*
  - (Repeat for words 2–5.)
e. (Repeat step d until firm.)

The third type of list consists of words that are easy to decode or words that the students have already learned. The teacher simply directs the students to read these lists.

Column 6

f. Find column 6. ✓
* (Teacher reference:)

1. early	3. thirsty
2. fuel	4. thirstier

g. Word 1. What word? (Signal.) *Early.*
* (Repeat for words 2–4.)
h. Let's read those words again.
* Word 1. What word? (Signal.) *Early.*
* (Repeat for words 2–4.)
i. (Repeat step h until firm.)

Individual Turns

(For columns 1–6: Call on individual students, each to read one to three words per turn.)

The next exercise in Lesson 52, Exercise 3, reviews the model sentence that was introduced in Exercise 1. Students say the sentence and answer questions about word meanings.

EXERCISE 3
VOCABULARY REVIEW

a. Here's the new vocabulary sentence: The smoke swirled in enormous billows.
* Everybody, say that sentence. Get ready. (Signal.) *The smoke swirled in enormous billows.*
* (Repeat until firm.)
* What word means **very, very large?** (Signal.) *Enormous.*
b. What word tells you that the clouds were swelling up? (Signal.) *Billows.*
* What word means that the smoke spun around and around? (Signal.) *Swirled.*

The following group reading activities appear in Lesson 16 of *Reading Mastery* Level 3. In Lesson 16—and most other lessons—the students read their *Textbook* stories aloud. Many of these stories are preceded by comprehension passages. The comprehension passages present background information for the stories. The students will make use of this information as they read the stories.

The students read the comprehension passage aloud. Individual students take turns reading two or three sentences each. As the students read the passage, the teacher presents comprehension questions from the *Presentation Book*. These questions teach a variety of comprehension, reference, and study skills.

B **More Facts About** Toads and Frogs

Toads and frogs are members of the same family. But toads are different from frogs. Here are some facts about how toads and frogs are different:
* Toads have skin that is rough and covered with warts.
* No toads have teeth, but some frogs have teeth.
* The back legs of toads are not as big or strong as the back legs of frogs.

EXERCISE 3
COMPREHENSION PASSAGE

a. Find part B in your textbook. ✓
* The information passage gives some facts about toads and frogs.
b. Everybody, touch the title. ✓
* (Call on a student to read the title.) [*More Facts About Toads and Frogs.*]
* Everybody, what's the title? (Signal.) *More Facts About Toads and Frogs.*
c. (Call on individual students to read the passage, each student reading two or three sentences at a time.)

More Facts About Toads and Frogs

  Toads and frogs are members of the same family. But toads are different from frogs. Here are some facts about how toads and frogs are different:
  Toads have skin that is rough and covered with warts.

* Everybody, what is a toad's skin covered with? (Signal.) *Warts.*
* Warts are like rough bumps. Everybody, do **frogs** have skin that is rough and covered with warts? (Signal.) *No.*

No toads have teeth, but some frogs have teeth.

* Everybody, listen to that fact again: No toads have teeth, but some frogs have teeth.

- Say that fact. Get ready. (Signal.) *No toads have teeth, but some frogs have teeth.*
- (Repeat until firm.)
- Do any toads have teeth? (Signal.) *No.*
- Do any frogs have teeth? (Signal.) *Yes.*

The back legs of toads are not as big or strong as the back legs of frogs.

- Everybody, whose back legs are stronger, toads' or frogs'? (Signal.) *Frogs'.*
- So which animal could jump farther, a toad or a frog? (Signal.) *A frog.*

After they finish the comprehension passage, the students read the main story aloud within decoding error limits that are specified in the teacher's script.

As the students read the story, the teacher presents comprehension questions from the *Presentation Book*. The comprehension questions in *Reading Mastery* Level 3 emphasize interpretive comprehension skills, reasoning skills, and study skills. In the sample selections from Lesson 16, the students interpret titles, infer story details, infer causes and effects, and predict outcomes.

c Goad Uses Her First Trick

Goad lived near Four Mile Lake. Down the road from the lake was a town. The name of that town was Toadsville. It was named Toadsville because so many people who visited the town had come to hunt for a big, smart, fast toad. And in the evening you could find hundreds of people sitting around Toadsville talking about Goad. First they would talk about some of the traps that had been made to catch Goad. Then they would tell how Goad escaped. One of their favorite stories is the one of the great big net.

Five hunters from Alaska had come to Four Mile Lake with a net that was nearly a mile wide. They waited until Goad was on a hill where there were no trees, just some white rocks. Then they flew over the hill in a plane and dropped the great big net over the hill. ✸ Goad was under the net. The five hunters rushed to the place where Goad had last been seen. But there was no Goad. There was some grass and five large white rocks. The hunters removed the net and began to go over every centimeter of the ground.

Suddenly, one of the hunters noticed that the biggest rock was moving. The biggest rock wasn't a rock at all. It was Goad.

She had moved near the other rocks. Then she had turned over on her back so that her white belly was showing. That belly looked like a white rock. Suddenly, she turned over. "There she is," one of the hunters yelled, but before the others could turn around, Goad hopped down the side of the hill and was gone.

MORE NEXT TIME

EXERCISE 4

STORY READING

a. Find part C in your textbook. ✓
- We're going to read this story two times. First you'll read it out loud and make no more than 6 errors. Then I'll read it and ask questions.
b. Everybody, touch the title. ✓
- (Call on a student to read the title.) *[Goad Uses Her First Trick.]*
- Everybody, what's Goad going to do in this story? (Signal.) *Her first trick.*

c. (Call on individual students to read the story, each student reading two or three sentences at a time.)

- (Correct errors: Tell the word. Direct the student to reread the sentence.)
- (If the group makes more than 6 errors, direct the students to reread the story.)

d. (After the group has read the selection making no more than 6 errors:)
Now I'll read the story and ask questions.

Goad Uses Her First Trick

Goad lived near Four Mile Lake. Down the road from the lake was a town. The name of that town was Toadsville. It was named Toadsville because so many people who visited the town had come to hunt for a big, smart, fast toad.

- Everybody, who is that big, smart, fast toad? (Signal.) *Goad.*

And in the evening you could find hundreds of people sitting around Toadsville talking about Goad. First they would talk about some of the traps that had been made to catch Goad. Then they would tell how Goad escaped. One of their favorite stories is the one of the great big net.

- How could you use a great big net to catch a toad? (Call on a student. Idea: *Drop it on top of the toad.*)

Five hunters from Alaska had come to Four Mile Lake with a net that was nearly a mile wide. They waited until Goad was on a hill where there were no trees, just some white rocks. Then they flew over the hill in a plane and dropped the great big net over the hill.
Goad was under the net. The five hunters rushed to the place where Goad had last been seen. But there was no Goad. There was some grass and five large white rocks. The hunters removed the net and began to go over every centimeter of the ground.

- The picture on the next page shows the hunters looking for Goad. You can see the trick that Goad is using. What is she doing? (Call on a student. Idea: *Pretending to be a rock.*)

Suddenly, one of the hunters noticed that the biggest rock was moving. The biggest rock wasn't a rock at all. It was Goad.
She had moved near the other rocks. Then she had turned over on her back so that her white belly was showing. That belly looked like a white rock. Suddenly she turned over. "There she is," one of the hunters yelled, but before the others could turn around, Goad hopped down the side of the hill and was gone.

MORE NEXT TIME

- Why didn't those hunters just grab her when she was hopping down the hill? (Call on a student. Idea: *Goad was too fast.*)

After the students finish the *Textbook* reading activities, they work independently in the *Workbook* and *Textbook*. The independent work includes items about the comprehension passage, story items, skill items, and review items.

The comprehension passage items and story items are based on the comprehension questions presented during the group reading. In this sample lesson, the students recall narrative details, classify objects, explain causes and effects, and infer narrative events. Story items in other lessons involve skills such as sequencing narrative events, inferring details, and interpreting motives.

The skill items teach vocabulary and reasoning skills. In this sample lesson, the students make comparisons.

The review items review previously taught facts and skills. In this sample lesson, the students review map-reading skills, measurement information, and facts about fleas and apple trees.

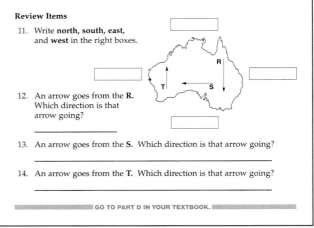

Review Items

11. Write **north, south, east,** and **west** in the right boxes.

12. An arrow goes from the **R.** Which direction is that arrow going?
_____

13. An arrow goes from the **S.** Which direction is that arrow going?
_____

14. An arrow goes from the **T.** Which direction is that arrow going?
_____

▩▩▩▩▩▩ GO TO PART D IN YOUR TEXTBOOK. ▩▩▩▩▩▩

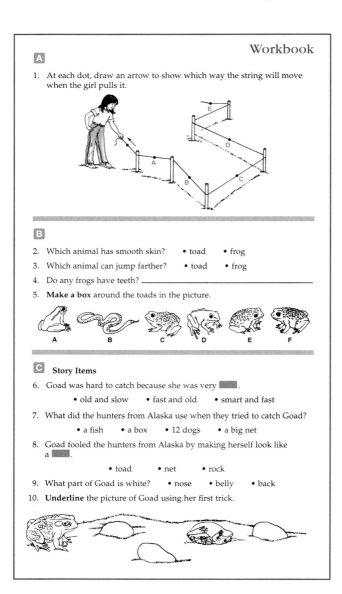

Workbook

A

1. At each dot, draw an arrow to show which way the string will move when the girl pulls it.

B

2. Which animal has smooth skin?   • toad   • frog
3. Which animal can jump farther?   • toad   • frog
4. Do any frogs have teeth? _____
5. **Make a box** around the toads in the picture.

  A   B   C   D   E   F

C Story Items

6. Goad was hard to catch because she was very ▮▮▮▮.
     • old and slow   • fast and old   • smart and fast
7. What did the hunters from Alaska use when they tried to catch Goad?
     • a fish   • a box   • 12 dogs   • a big net
8. Goad fooled the hunters from Alaska by making herself look like a ▮▮▮▮.
          • toad   • net   • rock
9. What part of Goad is white?   • nose   • belly   • back
10. **Underline** the picture of Goad using her first trick.

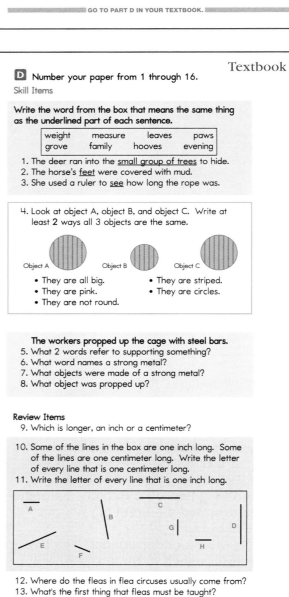

Textbook

D Number your paper from 1 through 16.
Skill Items

Write the word from the box that means the same thing as the underlined part of each sentence.

| weight | measure | leaves | paws |
| grove | family | hooves | evening |

1. The deer ran into the <u>small group of trees</u> to hide.
2. The horse's <u>feet</u> were covered with mud.
3. She used a ruler to <u>see</u> how long the rope was.

4. Look at object A, object B, and object C. Write at least **2** ways all 3 objects are the same.

Object A   Object B   Object C

• They are all big.   • They are striped.
• They are pink.   • They are circles.
• They are not round.

The workers propped up the cage with steel bars.
5. What 2 words refer to supporting something?
6. What word names a strong metal?
7. What objects were made of a strong metal?
8. What object was propped up?

Review Items
9. Which is longer, an inch or a centimeter?

10. Some of the lines in the box are one inch long. Some of the lines are one centimeter long. Write the letter of every line that is one centimeter long.
11. Write the letter of every line that is one inch long.

12. Where do the fleas in flea circuses usually come from?
13. What's the first thing that fleas must be taught?

14. What color are the flowers that apple trees make?
15. When do those flowers come out?
16. What grows in each place where there was a flower?

Reading Mastery Level 4

Reading Mastery Level 4 contains 140 daily lessons that emphasize problem-solving skills and reading in the content areas. Students in the program evaluate problems and solutions, learn facts about the world, and complete research projects. Many of the daily reading selections incorporate facts from science and social studies.

Classic Core Materials

For the teacher:

- *Presentation Books* (2)
- *Teacher's Guide*
- *Answer Key*

For the students:

- *Textbooks* (2)
- *Workbooks* (2)

The *Textbooks* contain stories, factual articles, and comprehension passages written especially for the program. All of the stories are serialized over a span of lessons. Most of the stories incorporate science facts and rules. Here is a partial listing of the contents of the *Textbooks*.

- **Old Henry and Tim**—The story of two geese who each help the other in his own way.
- **Oomoo, Oolak, and a Polar Bear**—A realistic story about Alaskan Eskimos.
- **Leonard the Inventor**—A realistic story about a boy who invents things.
- **A Trip Through the Solar System**—A science-fiction story.
- **Waldo the Animal Trainer**—A realistic story about a boy who trains animals.
- **Go Anywhere – See Anything**—An imaginative story about two children who can go anywhere and see anything.
- **Comprehension Passages**—Short passages that provide background information for the stories.
- **Factual Articles**—Articles about people and the world.

Sample Activities—Lesson 43

The following activities appear in Lesson 43 of *Reading Mastery* Level 4.

The students begin Lesson 43—and most other lessons—by working on model vocabulary sentences. These sentences contain selected vocabulary words. Students learn what each sentence means, practice saying the sentence, and respond to exercises about the meanings of specific words. In Lesson 43, Exercise 1, below, a new model sentence is introduced.

---

10. The patent attorney wrote an agreement.

EXERCISE 1

VOCABULARY

a. **Find the vocabulary sentences on page 352 in your textbook.** ✓
- Touch sentence 10. ✓
- This is a new vocabulary sentence. It says: The patent attorney wrote an agreement. Everybody, say that sentence. Get ready. (Signal.) *The patent attorney wrote an agreement.*
- Close your eyes and say the sentence. Get ready. (Signal.) *The patent attorney wrote an agreement.*
- (Repeat until firm.)
b. A **patent** is a license that says that only one person can make a particular product. New inventions are patented so that not everybody can make the product.
c. A patent **attorney** is a lawyer whose special job is getting patents for new inventions.
d. The sentence says the patent attorney wrote an **agreement.** An agreement is a paper that tells what two people promise to do. If people make an agreement, they shouldn't break the agreement. They should keep their promises.

---

e. Listen to the sentence again: The patent attorney wrote an agreement. Everybody say that sentence. Get ready. (Signal.) *The patent attorney wrote an agreement.*
f. Everybody, what word means **lawyer?** (Signal.) *Attorney.*
- What word names a license for somebody to be the only person who can make a product? (Signal.) *Patent.*
- What do we call a lawyer whose special job is getting patents for new inventions? (Signal.) *Patent attorney.*
- What word means **a promise made by people?** (Signal.) *Agreement.*
- (Repeat step f until firm.)

In Exercise 3 of Lesson 43, students read word lists. There are three types: lists of words that are difficult to decode, lists of words with common features, and lists of words that are easy to decode.

The teacher directs the students as they read these lists in unison. For each word in the lists whose meaning may not be familiar to the students, the teacher gives an explanation of the meaning. Finally, individual students take turns reading one to three words each.

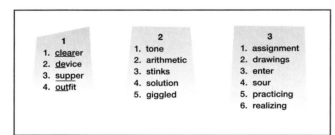

EXERCISE 3
READING WORDS
Column 1
a. Find lesson 43 in your textbook. ✓
- Touch column 1. ✓
- (Teacher reference:)

| 1. **clearer** | 3. **supper** |
| 2. **device** | 4. **outfit** |

- All these words have more than one syllable. The first part of each word is underlined.
b. Word 1. What's the underlined part? (Signal.) *clear.*
- What's the whole word? (Signal.) *Clearer.*
- Spell **clearer.** Get ready. (Tap for each letter.) *C-L-E-A-R-E-R.*
c. Word 2. What's the underlined part? (Signal.) *de.*
- What's the whole word? (Signal.) *Device.*
- Spell **device.** Get ready. (Tap for each letter.) *D-E-V-I-C-E.*
d. Word 3. What's the underlined part? *Supp.*
- What's the whole word? (Signal.) *Supper.*
- Spell **supper.** Get ready. (Tap for each letter.) *S-U-P-P-E-R.*
e. Word 4. What's the underlined part? (Signal.) *out.*
- What's the whole word? (Signal.) *Outfit.*
- Spell **outfit.** Get ready. (Tap for each letter.) *O-U-T-F-I-T.*
f. Let's read those words again.
- Word 1. What word? (Signal.) *Clearer.*
- (Repeat for: **2. device, 3. supper, 4. outfit.**)
g. (Repeat step f until firm.)

Column 2
h. Find column 2. ✓
- (Teacher reference:)

1. **tone**	4. **solution**
2. **arithmetic**	5. **giggled**
3. **stinks**	

i. Word 1. What word? (Signal.) *Tone.*
- Your tone of voice tells what you are feeling. I can say "What are you doing?" so it sounds like a question or so it sounds like I'm scolding you. Which tone of voice do you want to hear? (Call on a student. Student preference.)
- (Say "What are you doing?" using the selected tone of voice.)
j. Word 2. What word? (Signal.) *Arithmetic.*
- (Repeat for words 3–5.)
k. Let's read those words again.
- Word 1. What word? (Signal.) *Tone.*
- (Repeat for words 2–5.)
l. (Repeat step k until firm.)

Column 3

m. Find column 3. ✓
- (Teacher reference:)

1. assignment	4. sour
2. drawings	5. practicing
3. enter	6. realizing

n. Word 1. What word? (Signal.)
Assignment.
- (Repeat for words 2–6.)

o. Let's read those words again.
- Word 1. What word? (Signal.)
Assignment.
- (Repeat for words 2–6.)

p. (Repeat step o until firm.)

Individual Turns

(For columns 1–3: Call on individual students, each to read one to three words per turn.)

Some of the lessons are preceded by comprehension passages. The students read the comprehension passage aloud. Individual students take turns reading two or three sentences each. As the students read the passage, the teacher presents comprehension passages that provide background information for the stories.

Next the students read their *Textbook* stories aloud.

Leonard said, "Let me explain how it's going to work. It's dark outside. And it's dark in the living room of your house. But when you walk through the door to the living room, the light goes on automatically. The light stays on as long as you're in the living room. But when you leave the living room, the light goes off."

Leonard's mother shook her head. "That sounds far too difficult."

Grandmother Esther said, "It sounds difficult to you because you don't know how the electric eye works."

"The electric eye?" Leonard's mother asked.

Leonard said, "Here's how it works, Mom. There's a little beam of light that goes across the doorway to the living room. When you enter the room, you break the beam. When you break that beam, the light turns on. Then when you leave the room, you break the beam and the light goes off."

"Oh, my," Leonard's mother said. He could tell from her tone of voice that she didn't understand what he said.

"Good thinking," Grandmother Esther said, and slapped Leonard on the back. "That's a fine idea for an invention, a fine idea."

"Thank you," Leonard said.

Grandmother Esther made a sour looking face. Slowly she said, "There's one big problem with being a good inventor. You have to think of all the things that could go wrong."

"What could go wrong?" Leonard asked.

Grandmother Esther explained. "When you break the beam one time, the light goes on. When you break the beam the next time, the light goes off. When you break the beam the next time, the light goes on."

"Right," Leonard said.

"That's the problem," Grandmother Esther said. "What if two people walk into a dark room? When the first one goes into the room, the light will go on. Now the second person goes into the room. What happens to the light?"

"It goes off," Leonard said very sadly. He shook his head. "Now both people are in the dark, and my invention stinks."

"Wrong!" Grandmother Esther shouted. "Both people are in the dark, but your invention does not stink. Every invention has problems. An inventor has to look at these problems and try to solve them. But you must remember that inventing something is more than just getting an idea. You must work on that idea until it is a good idea. Then you must take that good idea and make it into a good invention. Just because there's a problem doesn't mean that you give up. You've got a great idea."

Leonard's mother said, "I have a great idea for an invention. It's a machine that . . ."

"Not now," Grandmother Esther said. "We're close to a <u>real</u> invention."

Leonard said, "I'll just have to think about the problem and try to figure out how to solve it."

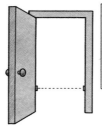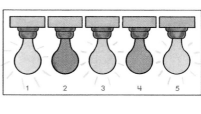

B   A Good Idea

The next evening, after supper, it happened. Leonard had no warning that it would happen. But it did. Everything in his mind suddenly came together and he had the idea for a great invention.

Here's how it happened: After supper, he went to his room to get a pencil. He was going to make some more drawings of ideas for inventions. When he started back to the kitchen, Grandmother Esther hollered at him, "Turn off the light in your room. Remember to save energy."

Leonard turned around, went back to his room, turned off the light, and stood there in the dark room. He felt the idea coming into his head. It got bigger and clearer and . . . "Hot dog!" he shouted. He shouted, "What an idea for an invention! Hot dog!"

He ran into the kitchen. "I've got it. What an idea! This is the best idea anybody ever had for an invention!"

His mother smiled. "I'll bet it's a machine that makes up a list of things you need at the store."

"Stop talking about that stupid machine," Grandmother Esther yelled from the other room. She ran into the kitchen. She was wearing her exercise outfit.

Grandmother Esther asked, "What's your idea, Leonard?"

The students must read the first part of each story within a decoding error limit that is specified in the teacher's script. As the students read, the teacher presents comprehension questions from the *Presentation Book*. After the students complete their oral reading, they read the rest of the story silently. The teacher presents another group of comprehension questions at the end of the silent reading.

The comprehension questions in *Reading Mastery* Level 4 emphasize reasoning skills and character analysis. In this sample lesson, the students evaluate problems and solutions, use rules to predict outcomes, interpret a character's feelings and motives, and predict a character's actions.

EXERCISE 4

STORY READING

a. Find part B in your textbook. ✓
• The error limit for group reading is 11 errors. Read carefully.
b. Everybody, touch the title. ✓
• (Call on a student to read the title.) [*A Good Idea.*]
• Everybody, what's the title? (Signal.) *A Good Idea.*
• (Call on individual students to read the story, each student reading two or three sentences at a time. Ask the specified questions as the students read.)

• (Correct errors: Tell the word. Direct the student to reread the sentence.)
• (If the group makes more than 11 errors, direct the students to reread the story.)

A Good Idea
The next evening, after supper, it happened. Leonard had no warning that it would happen. But it did. Everything in his mind suddenly came together and he had the idea for a great invention.

• What happened that evening? (Call on a student. Idea: *Leonard got an idea for a great invention.*)
• Everybody, did Leonard know that this would happen? (Signal.) *No.*

Here's how it happened: After supper, he went to his room to get a pencil. He was going to make some more drawings of ideas for inventions. When he started back to the kitchen, Grandmother Esther hollered at him, "Turn off the light in your room. Remember to save energy."
Leonard turned around, went back to his room, turned off the light, and stood there in the dark room. He felt the idea coming into his head. It got bigger and clearer and . . . "Hot dog!" he shouted.

• Why did he shout? (Call on a student. Ideas: *He was excited; he had an idea.*)
• How did he feel? (Call on a student. Ideas: *Happy, excited.*)

He shouted, "What an idea for an invention! Hot dog!"
He ran into the kitchen. "I've got it. What an idea! This is the best idea anybody ever had for an invention!"
His mother smiled. "I'll bet it's a machine that makes up a list of things you need at the store."
"Stop talking about that stupid machine," Grandmother Esther yelled from the other room. She ran into the kitchen. She was wearing her exercise outfit.

• Look at the picture on the next page. ✓
• What is Grandmother Esther wearing? (Call on a student. Ideas: *Her exercise outfit; purple sweatsuit.*)

Grandmother Esther asked, "What's your idea, Leonard?"

Leonard said, "Let me explain how it's going to work. It's dark outside. And it's dark in the living room of your house. But when you walk through the door to the living room, the light goes on automatically. The light stays on as long as you're in the living room. But when you leave the living room, the light goes off."

- Leonard explained how the invention would work. Listen to that part again:

  Leonard said, "Let me explain how it's going to work. It's dark outside. And it's dark in the living room of your house. But when you walk through the door to the living room, the light goes on automatically. The light stays on as long as you're in the living room. But when you leave the living room, the light goes off."
- What happens when you walk **into** the room? (Call on a student. Idea: *The light goes on.*)
- What happens when you **leave** the room? (Call on a student. Idea: *The light goes off.*)
- What kind of thing could make the lights go on and off automatically? (Call on a student. Idea: *An electric eye.*)

Leonard's mother shook her head. "That sounds far too difficult."

Grandmother Esther said, "It sounds difficult to you because you don't know how the electric eye works."

- Everybody, did Grandmother Esther know how Leonard was thinking of making the lights go on and off? (Signal.) *Yes.*
- What was he going to use? (Signal.) *An electric eye.*

"The electric eye?" Leonard's mother asked.

Leonard said, "Here's how it works, Mom. There's a little beam of light that goes across the doorway to the living room. When you enter the room, you break the beam. When you break that ✦ beam, the light turns on. Then when you leave the room, you break the beam and the light goes off."

"Oh, my," Leonard's mother said. He could tell from her tone of voice that she didn't understand what he said.

"Good thinking," Grandmother Esther said, and slapped Leonard on the back. "That's a fine idea for an invention, a fine idea."

"Thank you," Leonard said.

- Everybody, do you think she feels that the electric eye invention is the right idea? (Signal.) *Yes.*

Grandmother Esther made a sour looking face. Slowly she said, "There's one big problem with being a good inventor. You have to think of all the things that could go wrong."

"What could go wrong?" Leonard asked.

Grandmother Esther explained. "When you break the beam one time, the light goes on. When you break the beam the next time, the light goes off. When you break the beam the next time, the light goes on."

"Right," Leonard said.

"That's the problem," Grandmother Esther said. "What if two people walk into a dark room? When the first one goes into the room, the light will go on. Now the second person goes into the room. What happens to the light?"

"It goes off," Leonard said very sadly. He shook his head. "Now both people are in the dark, and my invention stinks."

- What happens when the first person enters the room? (Call on a student. Idea: *The light goes on.*)
- What happens when the second person enters the room? (Call on a student. Idea: *The light goes off.*)
- Everybody, is that the way Leonard wants it to work? (Signal.) *No.*

- Read the rest of the story to yourself and be ready to answer some questions. Remember, Leonard has just said that he thinks his invention stinks. Raise your hand when you're finished.

> **"Wrong!" Grandmother Esther shouted. "Both people are in the dark, but your invention does not stink. Every invention has problems. An inventor has to look at these problems and try to solve them. But you must remember that inventing something is more than just getting an idea. You must work on that idea until it is a good idea. Then you must take that good idea and make it into a good invention. Just because there's a problem doesn't mean that you give up. You've got a great idea."**
>
> **Leonard's mother said, "I have a great idea for an invention. It's a machine that . . ."**
>
> **"Not now," Grandmother Esther said. "We're close to a <u>real</u> invention."**
>
> **Leonard said, "I'll just have to think about the problem and try to figure out how to solve it."**

- (After all students have raised their hand:) Why did Leonard think that his invention stinks? (Call on a student. Idea: *Because it has problems.*)
- Everybody, did Grandmother Esther think it stinks? (Signal.) *No.*
- She told him that every new invention has problems. So what does the inventor have to do? (Call on a student. Idea: *Solve the problems.*)
- Leonard's mother said she had a great idea for an invention. What do you think it was? (Call on a student. Idea: *The automatic grocery list-writer.*)
- Everybody, is Leonard going to give up? (Signal.) *No.*
- What is he going to do? (Call on a student. Idea: *Think about the problem and try to solve it.*)

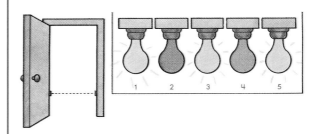

- Everybody, look at the picture. The picture shows Leonard's invention. The lights in the box show what will happen each time the beam of light is broken. When we start out, the light is **not on.** What will happen when the beam is broken **one time?** (Signal.) *The light will go on.*
- What happens when the beam is broken two times? (Signal.) *The light will go off.*
- Look at the picture in the box and get ready to tell me what will happen when the beam is broken **five** times. (Pause.) Get ready. (Signal.) *The light will go on.*
- Everybody, get ready to tell me what will happen when the beam is broken **four** times. (Pause.) Get ready. (Signal.) *The light will go off.*
- Can you figure out what will happen when the beam is broken **six** times? (Call on a student. Idea: *The light will go off.*)

After the students finish the *Textbook* reading activities, they work independently in their *Workbooks* and *Textbooks*. The independent work includes comprehension-passage items, story items, skill items, vocabulary items, and review items.

In some lessons, additional activities include fact games and complete special projects.

In this sample lesson, the students complete story items and review items. The story items are based on the comprehension questions presented during the group reading. For the story items, the students recall narrative details, evaluate problems and solutions, and use rules to predict outcomes. The review items review previously taught facts. In this sample lesson, the students review facts they have learned about prehistoric eras, animal behavior, and geographic locations.

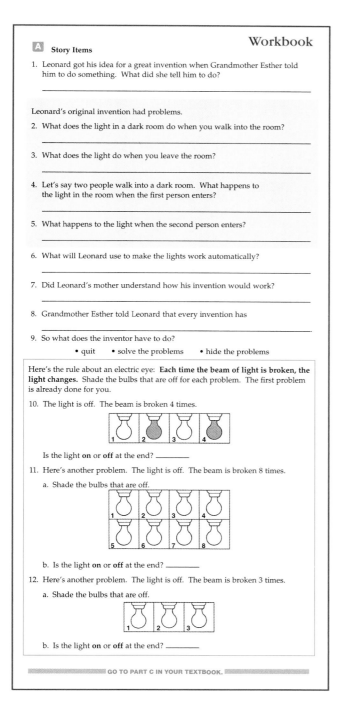

A Story Items   Workbook

1. Leonard got his idea for a great invention when Grandmother Esther told him to do something. What did she tell him to do?

_____

Leonard's original invention had problems.

2. What does the light in a dark room do when you walk into the room?

_____

3. What does the light do when you leave the room?

_____

4. Let's say two people walk into a dark room. What happens to the light in the room when the first person enters?

_____

5. What happens to the light when the second person enters?

_____

6. What will Leonard use to make the lights work automatically?

_____

7. Did Leonard's mother understand how his invention would work?

_____

8. Grandmother Esther told Leonard that every invention has

_____

9. So what does the inventor have to do?
    • quit   • solve the problems   • hide the problems

Here's the rule about an electric eye: **Each time the beam of light is broken, the light changes.** Shade the bulbs that are off for each problem. The first problem is already done for you.

10. The light is off. The beam is broken 4 times.

Is the light **on** or **off** at the end? _____

11. Here's another problem. The light is off. The beam is broken 8 times.
   a. Shade the bulbs that are off.

   b. Is the light **on** or **off** at the end? _____

12. Here's another problem. The light is off. The beam is broken 3 times.
   a. Shade the bulbs that are off.

   b. Is the light **on** or **off** at the end? _____

▓▓▓▓▓▓ GO TO PART C IN YOUR TEXTBOOK. ▓▓▓▓▓▓

C Number your paper from 1 through 24.   Textbook

Skill Items

Use the words in the box to write complete sentences.

device	outfit	solution	entered
impressed	mentioned	responded	vocabulary

1. They were ▓▓▓▓ by her large ▓▓▓▓.
2. He ▓▓▓▓ to her clever ▓▓▓▓.

Review Items

Here's how an electric eye at a store works.
3. When somebody walks in the door, the body stops the beam of light from reaching the ▓▓▓▓.
4. When the body stops the beam, what does the device do next?
5. What does that tell the shopkeeper?

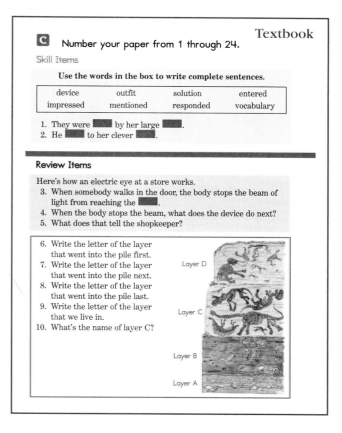

6. Write the letter of the layer that went into the pile first.
7. Write the letter of the layer that went into the pile next.
8. Write the letter of the layer that went into the pile last.
9. Write the letter of the layer that we live in.
10. What's the name of layer C?

Layer D
Layer C
Layer B
Layer A

11. Name the country that is just north of the United States.

12. Which letter shows where the United States is?
13. Which letter shows where Canada is?

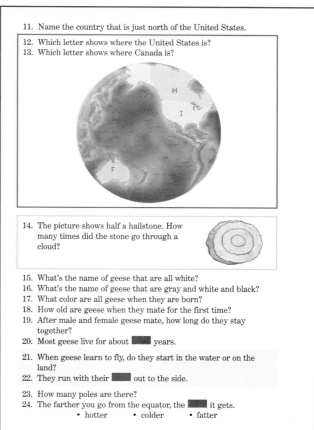

14. The picture shows half a hailstone. How many times did the stone go through a cloud?

15. What's the name of geese that are all white?
16. What's the name of geese that are gray and white and black?
17. What color are all geese when they are born?
18. How old are geese when they mate for the first time?
19. After male and female geese mate, how long do they stay together?
20. Most geese live for about ▓▓▓▓ years.
21. When geese learn to fly, do they start in the water or on the land?
22. They run with their ▓▓▓▓ out to the side.
23. How many poles are there?
24. The farther you go from the equator, the ▓▓▓▓ it gets.
    • hotter   • colder   • fatter

Reading Mastery Level 5

Reading Mastery Level 5 contains 120 daily lessons that emphasize literary analysis and extended writing. Students in the program read a wide range of classic and modern fiction and prose, including two full-length novels, and they learn how to analyze characters, settings, plots, and themes. The daily writing assignments focus on the meaning of literature and encourage students to think critically. Other program activities include making outlines, inferring word meaning from context, and interpreting reference materials.

Classic Core Materials

For the teacher:

- *Presentation Books* (2)
- *Teacher's Guide*
- *Answer Key*

For the students:

- *Textbooks* (2)
- *Workbook*

The *Textbooks* contain both classic and modern literature. Students read two full-length novels, as well as short stories, folktales, myths, factual articles, biographies, and poetry. Here is a partial listing:

- **Novels** by L. Frank Baum (*The Wonderful Wizard of Oz*) and Mark Twain (*The Prince and the Pauper*).
- **Short Stories** by well-known children's writers, including Jack London, Rudyard Kipling, and Hans Christian Andersen.
- **Folktales and Myths** from around the world, including "Beauty and the Beast," "The Miraculous Pitcher," and "The Golden Touch."
- **Factual Articles** about endangered species, Tudor England, the Yukon, animal migration, and other topics.
- **Biographies** of Jackie Robinson, Jane Addams, and Mark Twain.
- **Poetry** by Kathryn and Byron Jackson, Langston Hughes, and Harry Behn.

Sample Activities—Lesson 76

The following sample activities appear in the student *Textbook* and *Workbook* for Lesson 76 of *Reading Mastery* Level 5. (For a larger version of the student and teacher materials in Lesson 76, turn to the sample lesson at the back of this guide.)

As with every other lesson in Level 5, students begin Lesson 76 by reading in their *Textbooks*. Each *Textbook* lesson is divided into parts (part A, part B, part C, and so on). In part A of Lesson 76, students read different types of word lists aloud and practice using the words in sentences.

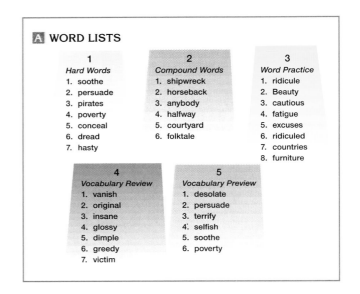

In part B, students read sentences that contain boldfaced vocabulary words. They then use context clues to determine the meanings of the vocabulary words.

B VOCABULARY FROM CONTEXT

1. There was nothing within a hundred miles of this lonely, **desolate** place.
2. She was good at talking people into doing things, but she could not **persuade** anybody to go to the beach with her.
3. The old house was frightening, and the sounds within it **terrified** me.
4. She seemed to be kind, but she was really very **selfish** and thought of nobody but herself.
5. He was so upset that nothing we could do would comfort or **soothe** him.
6. At first he was wealthy, but then he lost all his wealth and found himself in **poverty**.

In part C, students read a short "Story Background" passage that conveys important information about the story for Lesson 76, "Beauty and the Beast." The passage explains that the story is a folktale and describes differences between folktales and myths. The teacher asks questions from the *Presentation Book* as individual students take turns reading the passage aloud.

In part D, students read the first chapter of "Beauty and the Beast." The first part of the chapter is done aloud, with individual students reading a few sentences each. During this oral reading, the teacher asks a range of interpretative and analytical comprehension questions. Then students read the rest of the chapter silently. The teacher asks more comprehension questions when everyone has finished reading.

C STORY BACKGROUND

Folktales

The next story you will read is a folktale called "Beauty and the Beast." Like myths, folktales are old stories that people told aloud before someone wrote them down. But folktales are usually much newer than myths. The myths you have just read, for example, take place about three thousand years ago. In comparison, "Beauty and the Beast" takes place just a few hundred years ago.

Another difference is that myths usually include gods and goddesses, but folktales do not. Instead, folktales often have witches, wizards, or other kinds of magic.

"Beauty and the Beast" is one of the most famous folktales of all time. Many movies have been made of the story, and many writers have retold it in their own words. The story comes from France, a large country in Europe.

D READING

Beauty and the Beast
Chapter 1

Once upon a time there lived a merchant who was enormously rich. The merchant had six sons and six daughters, and he would let them have anything they wanted.

But one day their house caught fire and burned to the ground, with all the splendid furniture, books, pictures, gold, silver, and precious goods it contained. Yet this was only the beginning of their misfortune. Shortly after the fire, the merchant lost every ship he had upon the sea, either because of pirates, shipwrecks, or fire. Then he heard that the people who worked for him in distant countries had stolen his money. At last, he fell into great poverty.

All the merchant had after those misfortunes was a little cottage in a desolate place a hundred miles from the town in which he used to live. He moved into the cottage with his children. They were in de-

spair at the idea of leading such a different life. The cottage stood in the middle of a dark forest, and it seemed to be the most dismal place on earth.

The children had to cultivate the fields to earn their living. They were poorly clothed, and they missed the comforts and amusements of their earlier life. Only the youngest daughter tried to be brave and cheerful. She had also been sad at first, but she soon recovered her good nature. She set to work to make the best of things. But when she tried to persuade her sisters to join her in dancing and singing, they ridiculed her and said that this miserable life was all she was fit for. But she was far prettier and more clever than they were. She was so lovely that she was called Beauty.

After two years, their father received news that one of his ships, which he had believed to be lost, had come safely into port with a rich cargo. All the sons and daughters at once thought their poverty would be over, and they wanted to set out directly for the town. But their father was more cautious, so he decided to go by himself. Only Beauty had any doubt that they would soon be rich again. The other daughters gave their father requests for so many jewels and dresses that it would have taken a fortune to buy them. But Beauty did not ask for anything. Her father noticed her silence and said, "And what shall I bring for you, Beauty?"

"The only thing I wish for is to see you come home safely," she answered.

This reply angered her sisters, who thought she was accusing them of asking for costly things. But her father was pleased. Still, he told her to choose something.

"Well, dear Father," she said, "since you insist upon it, I want you to bring me a rose. I have not seen one since we came here, and I love them very much." ♦

So the merchant set out on horseback and reached the town as quickly as possible. But when he got there, he found out that his partners had taken the goods the ship had brought. So he found himself poorer than when he had left the cottage. He had only enough money to buy food on his journey home. To make matters worse, he left town during terrible weather. The storm was so bad that he was exhausted with cold and fatigue before he was halfway home. Night came on, and the deep snow and bitter frost made it impossible for the merchant's horse to carry him any further.

The merchant could see no houses or lights. The only shelter he could find was the hollow trunk of a great tree. He crouched there all night long. It was the longest night he had ever known. In spite of his weariness, the howling of the wolves kept him awake. And when the day broke, he was not much better off, for falling snow had covered up every path, and he did not know which way to turn.

At last, he made out some sort of path, and he started to follow it. It was rough and slippery, so he kept falling down. But the path soon became easier, and it led him to a row of trees that ended at a splendid castle. It seemed very strange to the merchant that no snow had fallen in the row of trees. Stranger still, the trees were fruit trees, and they were covered with apples and oranges. ✶

The merchant walked down the row of trees and soon reached the castle. He called, but nobody answered. So he opened the door and called again. Then he climbed

up a flight of steps and walked through several splendid rooms. The pleasant warmth of the air refreshed him, and he suddenly felt very hungry; but there seemed to be nobody in this huge palace who could give him anything to eat.

The merchant kept wandering through the deep silence of the splendid rooms. At last, he stopped in a room smaller than the rest, where a bright fire was burning next to a couch. The merchant thought this room must be prepared for someone, so he sat down to wait. But very soon he fell into a heavy sleep.

His extreme hunger wakened him after several hours. He was still alone, but

a good dinner had been set on a little table. The merchant had eaten nothing for an entire day, so he lost no time in beginning his meal, which was delicious. He wondered who had brought the food, but no one appeared.

After dinner, the merchant went to sleep again. He woke completely refreshed the next morning. There was still no sign of anybody, although a fresh meal of cakes and fruit was sitting on the little table at his elbow. The silence began to terrify the merchant, and he decided to search once more through the rooms. But it was no use. There was no sign of life in the palace. Not even a mouse could be seen.

After students finish the reading activities, they work independently in their *Textbooks* and *Workbooks*. In the *Textbook* exercises for Lesson 76, students write the main idea of a paragraph (part E), answer interpretative comprehension questions about the story (part F), and write a poem (part G).

Students write the answers to *Workbook* exercises in the *Workbook* itself. In Lesson 76, they answer literal comprehension questions about the story (part A), use vocabulary words in context (part B), sequence story events (part C), and review material from earlier lessons in the program (parts D and E).

A STORY DETAILS

Write the answers.

1. At the beginning of the story, how rich was the merchant?

2. How many children did the merchant have?

3. What happened to his house?

4. What kind of house did the family move into?

5. Before her father left for town, what did Beauty ask him to bring back?

6. What kinds of things did the other children ask for?

7. Where did the merchant sleep during the storm?

8. What was strange about the row of trees the merchant found?

9. Why was the palace so silent?

B VOCABULARY

Write the correct words in the blanks.

shrewd	calculate
witty	century
appetite	secure
inhabitant	sympathy
discontented	defeat

1. Lillian was so _____ with her job that she quit.

2. The wise man made many _____ decisions.

3. A _____ is a long time.

4. The experts could not _____ the number of stars in the sky.

5. She was glad to see the food because she had an enormous _____.

6. The cat was _____ from dogs as long as it stayed inside the house.

7. After the child fell, her mother held her and showed great _____.

E MAIN IDEA

For each paragraph, write a sentence that tells the complete main idea.

1. Saturday finally arrived. Janet took her camera out of her closet. Then she went outside to look for her friends. When she had found everybody, she told them to stand together on her porch. She looked through her camera and told everybody to stand closer together. Finally, she said, "Smile," and pressed the button on the camera. The camera went "click," and some of Janet's friends made faces.

2. William liked rowing boats. Last spring, William visited Swan Lake. He rented a rowboat for the whole day. He hopped into the boat and started to pull the oars. The boat started across the lake. William could see the boat rental place getting farther and farther away. William kept rowing. He looked at people fishing and at birds flying near the water. He had fun seeing how fast he could row. After a long time, he came to the opposite side of the lake.

F COMPREHENSION

Write the answers.

1. Why were most of the merchant's children greedy and spoiled?
2. Name at least three ways that Beauty was different from her sisters.
3. Why do you think Beauty asked her father for a rose?
4. Why did the merchant get lost on the way home?
5. Name at least three strange things about the palace.

G WRITING

What objects do you think are beautiful?
• Pick an object that you think is beautiful, such as a flower, a painting, or a river. Then write a poem about the object. Describe what the object looks like and tell why you think it's beautiful.

C SEQUENCING

Put the following events in the correct order by numbering them from **1** to **5**.

___ The merchant found a palace.

___ The merchant spent the night in a tree.

___ The merchant moved to a cottage.

___ The merchant's house burned down.

___ The merchant went back to the town.

D RELATED FACTS

Write which Greek god each statement describes. Choose **Hermes, Poseidon,** or **Zeus.**

1. The god of the sky

2. The god of the ocean

3. The god of travelers

E STORY REVIEW

Write whether each statement describes **The Miraculous Pitcher** or **The Golden Touch.**

1. Zeus appeared in this story.

2. The main character was a king.

3. One of the characters had a magic staff.

4. One of the characters was changed into a statue.

5. The story showed how evil greed can be.

6. The story showed why you should be kind to strangers.

Reading Mastery Level 6

Reading Mastery Level 6 contains 120 daily lessons that focus on literary language, reasoning strategies, and extended writing. The reading selections include novels, short stories, poems, factual articles, biographies, and a play. Students in the program interpret complex sentence forms, figurative language, and literary irony; they also identify contradictions and faulty logic. In addition, students write a wide variety of essays, dialogues, short stories, and poems.

Classic Core Materials

For the teacher:

- *Presentation Books* (2)
- *Teacher's Guide*
- *Answer Key*

For the students:

- *Textbooks* (2)
- *Workbook*

The *Textbooks* contain both classic and modern literature. Students read a full-length novel by Mark Twain and three novellas, as well as short stories, a folktale, a myth, factual articles, poetry, biographies, and a play. Here is a partial listing:

- **Novels and Novellas** by Mark Twain (*Tom Sawyer*), Homer (*The Odyssey*), Frances Hodgson Burnett (*Sara Crewe*), and Jack London (*The Cruise of the* Dazzler).
- **Short Stories** by well-known writers, including Robert McCloskey, O. Henry, Guy de Maupassant, and Sarah Orne Jewett.
- **Folktales and Myths** from around the world, including "The Table, the Donkey, and the Stick," and "Persephone."
- **Factual Articles** about American history, the apprentice system, and San Francisco Bay.
- **Biographies** of Harriet Tubman and Jack London.
- **Poetry** by Walt Whitman, William Wordsworth, and Ernest Thayer.

Sample Activities—Lesson 57

The following sample activities appear in the student *Textbook* and *Workbook* for Lesson 57 of *Reading Mastery* Level 6. (For a larger version of the student and teacher materials in Lesson 57, turn to the sample lesson at the back of this guide.)

As with every other lesson in Level 6, students begin Lesson 57 by reading in their *Textbooks*. Each *Textbook* lesson is divided into parts (part A, part B, part C, and so on). In part A of Lesson 57, students read different types of word lists aloud.

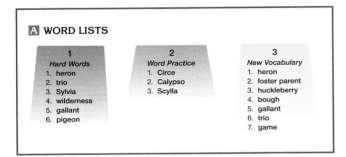

A WORD LISTS

1	2	3
Hard Words	*Word Practice*	*New Vocabulary*
1. heron	1. Circe	1. heron
2. trio	2. Calypso	2. foster parent
3. Sylvia	3. Scylla	3. huckleberry
4. wilderness		4. bough
5. gallant		5. gallant
6. pigeon		6. trio
		7. game

In part B, students read vocabulary definitions aloud and practice using the vocabulary words in context.

B VOCABULARY DEFINITIONS

1. **heron**—*Herons* are birds that wade through water and eat frogs and fish. Herons usually have tall, thin legs and a long, S-shaped neck. The picture shows a *white heron*.
   • Describe a heron.
2. **foster parent**—A *foster parent* is somebody who brings up a child but is not the child's real parent.

   • What do we call somebody who brings up a child but is not the child's real parent?
3. **huckleberry**—A *huckleberry* is a small purple or black berry that grows on bushes.
   • What is a huckleberry?
4. **bough**—A *bough* of a tree is a branch of the tree.
   • What is a branch of a tree?
5. **gallant**—Somebody who is *gallant* is brave and noble.
   • What's another way of saying *He was a noble warrior*?
6. **trio**—A *trio* is a group of three.
   • What's another way of saying *A group of three went to the river*?
7. **game**—Wild animals that are hunted are called *game*.
   • What do we call wild animals that are hunted?

In part C, students read the first part of "A White Heron," a classic short story by Sarah Orne Jewett. The story includes a focus question that draws attention to a central theme. Students have the option of reading the first part of the story aloud; the second part is always read silently. After the students finish reading, the teacher asks the comprehension questions.

C READING

A White Heron
*by Sarah Orne Jewett**
Part 1

Focus Question: How did Sylvia feel about living on her foster mother's farm?

The woods were filled with shadows one June evening, but a bright sunset still glimmered faintly among the trunks of the trees. A girl named Sylvia was driving a cow from the pasture to her home. Sylvia had spent more than an hour looking for the cow and had finally found her hiding behind a huckleberry bush.

Sylvia and the cow were going away from the sunset and into the dark woods. But they were familiar with the path, and the darkness did not bother them.

Sylvia wondered what her foster mother, Mrs. Tilley, would say because they were so late. But Mrs. Tilley knew how difficult it was to find the cow. She had chased the beast many times herself. As she waited, she was only thankful that Sylvia could help her. Sylvia seemed to love the out-of-doors, and Mrs. Tilley thought that being outdoors was a good change for an orphan girl who had grown up in a town.

The companions followed the shady road. The cow took slow steps, and the girl took very fast ones. The cow stopped at the brook to drink, and Sylvia stood still and waited. She let her bare feet cool them-

selves in the water while the great twilight moths struck softly against her. She waded on through the brook as the cow moved away, and she listened to the waterbirds with pleasure.

There was a stirring in the great boughs overhead. They were full of little birds that seemed to be wide awake and going about their business. Sylvia began to feel sleepy as she walked along. However, it was not much farther to the house, and the air was soft and sweet.

She was not often in the woods so late as this. The darkness made her feel as if she were a part of the gray shadows and the moving leaves. She was thinking how long it seemed since she had first come to her foster mother's farm a year ago. Sylvia wondered if everything was still going on in the noisy town just the same as when she had lived there. ◆

It seemed to Sylvia that she had never been alive at all before she came to live at her foster mother's farm. It was a beautiful place to live, and she never wished to go back to the town. The thought of the children who used to chase and frighten her made her hurry along the path to escape from the shadows of the trees.

_____
* *Adapted for young readers*

After students finish the reading activities, they work independently in their *Textbooks* and *Workbooks*. In the *Textbook* exercises for Lesson 57, students make inferences (part D), complete deductions (part E), review vocabulary words (part F), answer interpretative comprehension questions about the story (part G), and write an essay (part H).

Suddenly, she was horror-struck to hear a clear whistle not very far away. It was not a bird's whistle. It sounded more like a boy's. Sylvia stepped aside into the bushes, but she was too late. The whistler had discovered her, and he called out in a cheerful voice, "Hello, little girl, how far is it to the road?"

Trembling, Sylvia answered quietly, "A long distance."

She did not dare to look at the tall young man, who carried a gun over his shoulder. But Sylvia came out of the bushes and again followed the cow, while the young man walked alongside her.

"I have been hunting for some birds," the stranger said kindly, "and I have lost my way. Don't be afraid," he added gallantly. "Speak up and tell me what your name is and whether you think I can spend the night at your house and go out hunting early in the morning." ✳

Sylvia was more alarmed than before. Would her foster mother blame her for this? She hung her head, but she managed to answer "Sylvia" when her companion again asked her name.

Mrs. Tilley was standing in the doorway when the trio came into view. The cow gave a loud moo as if to explain the situation.

Mrs. Tilley said, "Yes, you'd better speak up for yourself, you naughty old cow! Where'd she hide herself this time, Sylvia?" But Sylvia kept silent.

The young man stood his gun beside the door and dropped a heavy gamebag next to it. Then he said good evening to Mrs. Tilley. He repeated his story and asked if he could have a night's lodging.

"Put me anywhere you like," he said. "I must be off early in the morning, before day, but I am very hungry indeed. Could you give me some milk?"

"Dear sakes, yes," said Mrs. Tilley. "You might do better if you went out to the main road, but you're welcome to what we've got. I'll milk the cow right now, and you make yourself at home. Now step round and set a plate for the gentleman, Sylvia!"

Sylvia promptly stepped. She was glad to have something to do, and she was hungry herself.

D INFERENCE

Write the answers for items 1–8.

You have to answer different types of questions about the passages you read. Some questions are answered by words in the passage. Other questions are *not* answered by words in the passage. You have to figure out the answer by making a deduction.

The following passage includes both types of questions.
More about Ecology

Two hundred years ago, many people were not concerned with ecology. They believed there was no end to the different types of wildlife, so they killed wild animals by the hundreds of thousands. When we look back on these killings, we may feel shocked. But for the people who lived two hundred years ago, wild animals seemed to be as plentiful as weeds.

Because of these killings, more than a hundred types of animals have become extinct since 1800. An animal is extinct when there are no more animals of that type.

One type of extinct animal is the passenger pigeon. At one time, these birds were so plentiful that flocks of them used to blacken the sky. Now the passenger pigeon is gone forever. Think of that. You will never get to see a living passenger pigeon or any of the other animals that have become extinct. The only place you can see those animals is in a museum, where they are stuffed and mounted.

1. Are house cats extinct?
2. Is that question answered by **words** or a **deduction**?
3. Name one type of extinct animal.
4. **Words** or **deduction**?
5. How many types of animals have become extinct since 1800?
6. **Words** or **deduction**?
7. The dodo bird is extinct. How many animals of that type are alive today?
8. **Words** or **deduction**?

E DEDUCTIONS

Write the answers about the deductions.
Oliver believed that if he studied, he would pass the test. Oliver studied for the test.
1. So, what did Oliver believe would happen?

Nadia believed that if you ate an apple a day you would stay healthy. Nadia ate an apple every day.
2. So, what did Nadia believe would happen?

F VOCABULARY REVIEW

unprecedented
maneuver
devoted
spurn
endured
regard

For each item, write the correct word.
1. When you move skillfully, you ▬▬▬.
2. When you consider something, you ▬▬▬ it.
3. Something that has never occurred before is ▬▬▬.

G COMPREHENSION

Write the answers.
1. How did Sylvia feel about living on her foster mother's farm?
2. Why didn't Sylvia like the town?
3. Why do you think Sylvia didn't dare to look at the young man?
4. How do you think Sylvia feels about hunting? Explain your answer.
5. What do you think will happen in the next part of the story?

H WRITING

Where would you rather live, on a farm or in a town?

Write an essay that explains your answer. Try to answer the following questions:
• What are the advantages of living on a farm?
• What are the disadvantages of living on a farm?
• What are the advantages of living in a town?
• What are the disadvantages of living in a town?
• Where would you rather live? Why?
Make your essay at least sixty words long.

Students write the answers to *Workbook* exercises in the *Workbook* itself. In Lesson 57, they answer literal comprehension questions about the story (part A), use vocabulary words in context (part B), identify different types of figurative language (part C), complete deductions (part D), distinguish characters by trait (part E), and make comparisons (part F).

A STORY DETAILS

Write or circle the answers.

1. Sylvia was __ who lived on a farm.
   • a vacationer   • a farmhand   • an orphan

2. Where had Sylvia lived before coming to the farm?
   _____

3. Sylvia thought she had never been __ at all before coming to the farm.
   • scared   • alive   • punished

4. Which place did Sylvia enjoy more, the town or the farm?
   _____

5. How had the children in town treated Sylvia?
   _____

6. What was the young man doing in the woods?
   _____

7. Was Sylvia bold or shy?
   _____

8. What was the name of the person who owned the farm?
   _____

9. That person was Sylvia's __.
   • employer   • mother   • foster parent

B VOCABULARY

Write the correct words in the blanks.

regarded	suitable
appealed	humiliating
unprecedented	maneuvered

1. The starving boy _____ to the sympathy of the crowd.

2. They _____ the criminal as a dangerous person.

3. He _____ the shopping cart past the fallen cans.

4. The pitcher made an _____ number of strikeouts.

C FIGURATIVE LANGUAGE

For each statement, write **simile, metaphor,** or **exaggeration.**

1. Her face was like a pale star.
   _____

2. The apartment was a prison.
   _____

3. The day was like a dream.
   _____

D DEDUCTIONS

Complete each deduction.
Every element has an atomic weight. Argon is an element.

1. What's the conclusion about argon?
   _____
   _____

Horses eat grass. A palomino is a horse.

2. What's the conclusion about a palomino?
   _____
   _____

E CHARACTER TRAITS

Write whether each phrase describes **Sylvia, Mrs. Tilley,** or **the stranger.**

1. Very shy
   _____

2. Whistled loudly
   _____

3. An orphan
   _____

4. Owned a farm
   _____

5. Felt like a part of the woods
   _____

6. Hunted for animals
   _____

F COMPARISONS

Write **Odyssey** if the event occurred in *The Odyssey*. Write **Yarn** if the event occurred in "Mystery Yarn."

1. Telemachus was one of the suitors.
   _____

2. Telemachus helped defeat the suitors.
   _____

3. The suitors took a test that involved unwinding string.
   _____

4. The suitors took a test that involved a bow and arrow.
   _____

GO TO PART D IN YOUR TEXTBOOK.

Testing and Management

The six *Reading Mastery* Classic placement tests determine the level in which students should be placed. The in-program mastery tests measure student progress within each level. The specifications for each test provide instructions for administration, student testing material, record-keeping charts, and remedial exercises.

Placement Tests

The *Reading Mastery* Classic sequence may begin in either K or 1. To ensure accurate placement, each level of the series includes a placement test. There are six placement tests. There is no separate placement test for *Fast Cycle*. The placement test for *Reading Mastery I* can be used to determine if beginning students should be placed in *Fast Cycle* or Level I. These placement tests should be administered at the beginning of the school year. The placement test results will provide you with

- information about the students' decoding and comprehension skills,
- a means of identifying which students should be placed in another level of the *Reading Mastery* sequence,
- guidelines for grouping the students.

Copies of the placement tests and accompanying instructions appear on pages 67–81 of this guide as well as in the *Teacher's Guides.* These pages may be reproduced for classroom use.

In-Program Mastery Tests

The *Reading Mastery* series is designed so that the students are constantly tested on their reading skills as they progress through each level of the series. Every student's decoding skills are periodically measured through rate-and-accuracy checkouts. For these checkouts, the student reads a passage aloud as you record the student's decoding errors. Comprehension, reference, and study skills are measured through the daily independent work. Because the independent work is directly related to other program material, it serves as a continuous test of each student's skill mastery. You check the independent work every day and use a chart to keep track of each student's performance.

You can use the rate-and-accuracy checkouts and the independent work to identify students who need remedial help. The *Teacher's Guides* contain specific remedial procedures for students who do not perform well on these exercises. These procedures include a review of program material and additional practice with specific skills. The procedures can be used with individual students or with an entire group.

In-program tests are integrated into the program components in Levels I through 4. These criterion-referenced tests are scheduled intermittently in Level I, every fifth lesson in Level II, and every tenth lesson in Levels 3 and 4. Optional *Management Handbooks* are available as separate components for Levels 5 and 6. Each test item measures student mastery of a specific skill taught in the *Reading Mastery* series.

Grouping the Students

Reading Mastery can be presented either to small groups of students or to the entire class. In general, Levels I through 4 should be presented to small groups of students, while Levels 5 and 6 should be presented to the entire class.

Small-group instruction offers several advantages. If you use small-group instruction, the students can be grouped according to their ability levels: above-average, average, below-average. This homogeneous grouping will allow you to spend more time with the below-average students, who will need the most help. You can use the placement test results as a guideline for grouping the students.

Small-group instruction also allows you to monitor individual performance more closely. In small groups, individual students will have more opportunities to read aloud and to answer your questions. The students will also get a better view of any material presented. This is particularly important in *Reading Mastery I* and *II*, where you often point to pictures, words, and letters in the *Presentation Books.*

Small-group instruction is simple with *Reading Mastery* because you can teach one group of students while the rest of the students are doing their independent work. Ideally, for *Reading Mastery* Levels I and II, the class should be divided into three groups: above-average, average, and below-average. The below-average group should be the smallest. For *Reading Mastery* Levels 3 and 4, the class can be divided into just two groups: one for the below-average students and another for the rest of the class. *Reading Mastery* Levels 5 and 6 are usually presented to the entire class, but they can also be presented to small groups.

Scheduling the Reading Period

Generally, one reading lesson of *Reading Mastery* should be presented on each day of the school year. Every lesson is divided into three parts: group instruction, independent work, and workcheck. The group instruction usually requires thirty minutes; the independent work, between twenty and thirty minutes; the workcheck, ten minutes. The students should generally complete the independent work immediately after finishing the group instruction. However, they can also complete the independent work later in the day or even as homework.

The following chart shows one possible schedule for a *Reading Mastery* class with two groups of students.

	Group A	Group B
8:45–9:15	group instruction	
9:15–9:45	independent work	group instruction
9:45–10:15	workcheck	independent work
10:15–10:25		workcheck

Note: Spelling lessons (Levels I–3) are not to be presented as part of the reading lessons. Present them at a different time.

Motivating the Students

Reading Mastery is designed so that every student can succeed. Each lesson is a series of tasks or exercises. The students are able to succeed on each and every task, and their success is consistently rewarded. As soon as the students learn a new skill in one task, they apply that skill in another task and review it in still another. This constant application and review provides a consistent reward for learning. Students are motivated to learn each new skill because they know that they will soon be using that skill.

The programs also provide additional incentives for learning. In *Reading Mastery I* and *II*, the students can earn stars for reading well. In selected lessons, the teacher calls on individual students to read a story aloud. The student earns stars if he or she is able to read within a specific rate and error limit. The teacher keeps a permanent record of these stars.

Teaching Techniques

Arranging the Classroom

The classroom should be arranged differently for different levels of the program.

In *Reading Mastery I* and *II,* you will usually be presenting the program to small groups of students. The group that is being taught should be seated in a small semicircle in front of you. The students should sit on chairs, not at desks, and you should be within touching distance of every student. Every student in the group must be able to see the pictures or words that you present from the *Presentation Book.* The lowest performers in the group should be seated directly in front of you where you can monitor them closely.

Reading Mastery Levels 3 and 4 are usually presented to somewhat larger groups of students. The group that is being taught should face you. The students may sit at their desks or simply on chairs. The group can be arranged in any form as long as all students are facing you. The lowest performers should be seated directly in front of you.

Reading Mastery Levels 5 and 6 are usually presented to the entire class. The class should be facing you and the students should be at their desks. The lowest performers should be seated directly in front of you.

Using the Presentation Books

The *Presentation Books* contain complete scripts for presenting every lesson in *Reading Mastery.* The scripts are carefully written so that all instruction is clear and unambiguous. The program will be most effective if the scripts are followed closely.

The *Presentation Books* have several typefaces. The following typefaces are used in *Reading Mastery I* and *II.*

- This red type indicates what you say.
- This black type indicates what you do.
- *This italic type indicates the students' answers.*

The following typefaces are used in *Reading Mastery* Levels 3, 4, 5, and 6.

- What you say appears in blue type.
  You say this.
- What you do appears in parentheses.
  (You do this.)
- The responses of the students are in italics.
  Students say this.

Pacing the Lesson

Present the daily lessons at a lively pace. Fast pacing offers several advantages.

- Fast pacing generates student interest. Students are likely to pay attention if the lesson is presented at a lively pace.
- Fast pacing encourages student achievement. With fast pacing, you can cover more material and the students can receive more practice.
- Fast pacing keeps the students thinking. If a lesson is presented slowly, the students' minds may wander. With fast pacing, the students are constantly thinking, and they are unlikely to become distracted.
- Fast pacing reduces management problems. With fast pacing, the students are involved in their work and unlikely to misbehave.

To set a fast pace, you should move quickly, but you should not rush the students into making mistakes. Experience will show you the pace that is appropriate for each group. You should read over the material before presenting it. Fast pacing is easier if you do not have to refer to the *Presentation Book* for every word.

Using Signals

For many of the tasks in *Reading Mastery,* the students must answer aloud and in unison. This group response is very important because

- every student must initiate a response,
- every student is able to practice the task,
- you can monitor every student,
- you can hear any incorrect answers and correct them immediately.

For the students to answer simultaneously, you must use a signal. The signal eliminates the problem of one student leading the rest of the group.

There are two basic types of signals: visual and auditory. The visual signals are used when the students are looking at you or at the *Presentation Book.* You signal the students by making some type of hand motion (quickly dropping your hand, touching a word or picture, slashing under a word). Auditory signals are used in all levels. The students answer on signal as they read word lists, stories, and skill exercises. Auditory signals are used for these exercises because the students are looking at what they are reading, not at you. You can use either a foot tap, a clap, a finger snap, or a tap on a desk as an auditory signal.

You should use the following procedure for both visual and auditory signals.

1. Ask the specified question.
2. Pause for about one second.
3. Give the auditory or visual signal.
4. Listen to the group response and correct any errors.
5. Move quickly to the next question.

The one-second pause is very important. It clearly separates the question from the signal and ensures that every student sees or hears the signal. The pause should always last for about one second. When the pause is of a consistent length, the group is able to answer more effectively.

Praising the Students

The students will work harder if they receive praise for their work. Each lesson provides many opportunities for praise. You can praise the students when they learn a new sound, when they read lists of words, or when they read a story without making any errors. You can also praise students when they behave well and when they work particularly hard.

Praise should be simple and positive. You can say things such as, "Great. You read the entire list without making any mistakes," or "Good talking. I could hear everybody." The students are especially reinforced when you repeat a correct answer; for example, "Yes, that word is **am.**"

Praise should be an integral part of your presentation, but don't overdo it. Every statement of praise should clearly result from a specific student action. If praise is indiscriminate and undeserved, it will lose all meaning for the students. Generally, students in the lower levels of the program will require more praise than students in the upper levels.

Correcting Mistakes

The *Reading Mastery* programs include correction procedures for many of the mistakes that the students are likely to make. These mistakes fall into two categories: general and specific. The general mistakes include not paying attention and not answering on signal. The specific mistakes include misidentifying words and giving the wrong answers to questions.

General Mistakes

The general mistakes are most likely to occur when students are beginning the program. It is very important to correct these mistakes as soon as they occur so that students do not fall into bad habits.

In *Reading Mastery I* and *II,* the students must always pay attention when you are pointing to letters or words in the *Presentation Book.* If a student is not paying attention, use the following procedure.

1. Look at the student.
2. Say, "Watch my finger. Let's try it again."
3. Repeat the question as soon as the student is paying attention.
4. Return to the beginning of the task.

Variations of this procedure can be used whenever a student is not paying attention. You should always look at the student, tell the student to pay attention, repeat the question, and then return to the beginning of the task.

If a student is paying attention, but does not answer a question, you should use the following procedure.

1. Look at the student.
2. Say, "I have to hear everybody."
3. Repeat the question.
4. Return to the beginning of the task.

Every student must answer exactly on signal. A student who does not answer on signal may begin to depend on the other students for the correct answers. The correction procedure shows the students that you expect everyone to answer on signal.

If a student answers early or late, you should use the following procedure.

1. Look at the student.
2. Say, "You're early," or "You're late."
3. Repeat the question until all the students answer on signal.
4. Return to the beginning of the exercise.

By requiring a simultaneous response, you eliminate the problem of one student leading and the others following. When the students answer simultaneously, they have to think for themselves, and they will pay closer attention to you.

In all of these procedures, you must first correct the mistake and then return to the beginning of the exercise. By repeating the task, you demonstrate to the students that mistakes will not be ignored. The students must work on a task from beginning to end until they get it right. If general mistakes are properly corrected in the early lessons of a level, the students will make far fewer mistakes in the later lessons.

Specific Mistakes

When students misidentify a word or give a wrong answer, they are making a specific mistake. Many of the exercises in the *Presentation Books* contain correction procedures for specific mistakes. There are two basic types of correction procedures for specific mistakes. The first type is the *model-lead-test-retest* procedure. The second type is the *process-test-retest* procedure.

Here is an example of the *model-lead-test-retest* procedure.

```
To correct:
If the children do not say aaa:                 a
1. aaa.
2. Touch the first ball of the arrow. Say it with
   me. Get ready. Move quickly to the second
   ball of the arrow. Hold for two seconds. Say
   aaa with the children. aaa.
3. Touch the first ball of the arrow. Your turn.
   Get ready. Move quickly to the second ball
   of the arrow. Hold for two seconds. aaa.
```

In step 1, you *model* the correct answer. In step 2, you *lead* the students by saying the correct answer with them. (Sometimes, the *lead* step is not used.) In step 3, you *test* the students by having them say the correct answer by themselves. At a later point in the lesson, you *retest* the students by presenting the exercise again.

Here is an example of the *process-test-retest* procedure.

```
To correct:
1. Everybody, sound out the word. Touch each
   sound as the children sound out the word.
2. What word? (Signal.)             a m
```

In step 1, the students use a particular *process* to correct their mistakes. In this case, the process is to sound out the word. In step 2, you *test* the students by asking, What word? At a later point in the lesson, you *retest* the student by presenting the exercise again.

The specific correction procedures typically appear when a new skill is introduced because that is when the students are most likely to make mistakes. If the students are properly corrected at this time, they are unlikely to make mistakes when the skill appears in subsequent exercises. Nevertheless, you should memorize the correction procedure for a particular skill so that it can be administered at any time.

Teaching to Mastery

Every skill in *Reading Mastery* should be taught to mastery. When a skill is taught to mastery, every student in the group is able to perform the skill independently, without making any mistakes.

Teaching to mastery is of critical importance because the students are constantly applying each new skill. When a skill is taught to mastery, the students are able to apply the skill and are prepared to learn related skills. By teaching every skill to mastery, you ensure that each student is able to succeed throughout the program.

Practice Scripts

This section contains representative teacher presentation scripts from each level of the *Reading Mastery* Classic series. If you will be teaching *Reading Mastery,* you should practice the appropriate scripts before presenting the program to your students. You can practice these scripts on your own, with another teacher, or at a training session conducted by an experienced trainer.

To practice a script or a lesson, first read each script carefully and become familiar with it. Then present the script aloud several times, with only brief glances at the actual text. During these presentations, you should execute the proper signals and develop a rapid pace. Finally present the script to another person, who will play the role of the student. This "student" can then answer on signal and can also make intentional errors that you have to correct.

You should practice the scripts that are relevant to the program level you will be teaching. The following chart shows the practice scripts that are relevant to each level.

Level	Practice Scripts
I	1, 2, 3, 4, 5, 6
II	3, 4, 5, 6, 7
Fast Cycle	1, 2, 3, 4, 5, 6, 7
3	8, 9
4	8, 9
5	8, 9
6	8, 9, 10

If time permits, you should practice the remaining scripts. This additional practice will give you a valuable perspective on the entire program.

Full lesson scripts appear at the end of this guide.

Practice Scripts	Level						
	I	II	FC	3	4	5	6
Script 1 - Sounds	◆		◆				
Script 2 - Sounds	◆		◆				
Script 3 - Sounds	◆	◆	◆				
Script 4 - Word Reading	◆	◆	◆				
Script 5 - Word Reading	◆	◆	◆				
Script 6 - Story Reading	◆	◆	◆				
Script 7 - Story Reading		◆	◆				
Script 8 - Story Reading				◆	◆	◆	◆
Script 9 - Reading Words				◆	◆	◆	◆
Script 10 - Metaphors							◆

Practice Script 1

The following script appears in Lesson 4 of *Reading Mastery I*. The script introduces the sound **mmm.**

SOUNDS

TASK 5 Introducing the new sound mmm as in mat

a. Touch the first ball of the arrow. Here's a new sound. My turn to say it. When I move under the sound, I'll say it. I'll keep on saying it as long as I touch under it. Get ready. *Move quickly to the second ball of the arrow. Hold for two seconds.* **mmm.**

b. Touch the first ball of the arrow. My turn again. Get ready. *Move quickly to the second ball of the arrow. Hold for two seconds.* **mmm.**

c. Touch the first ball of the arrow. My turn again. Get ready. *Move quickly to the second ball of the arrow. Hold for two seconds.* **mmm.**

d. Touch the first ball of the arrow. Your turn. When I move under the sound, you say it. Keep on saying it as long as I touch under it. Get ready. *Move quickly to the second ball of the arrow. Hold for two seconds.* *mmm.* **Yes, mmm.**

To correct
If the children do not say *mmm:*
1. **mmm.**
2. Touch the first ball of the arrow. Say it with me. Get ready. *Move quickly to the second ball of the arrow. Hold for two seconds. Say* **mmm** *with the children.* *mmm.*
3. Touch the first ball of the arrow. Your turn. Get ready. *Move quickly to the second ball of the arrow. Hold for two seconds.* *mmm.*

---

e. Touch the first ball of the arrow. Again. Get ready. *Move quickly to the second ball of the arrow. Hold for two seconds.* *mmm.* **Yes, mmm.**
f. Repeat *e* until firm.
g. Call on different children to do *d.*
h. Good saying **mmm.**

Description

In steps a–c, you model the correct way to say the sound. In step d, you test the students by having them say the sound. Step d also includes a correction procedure. In steps e and f, you continue to test the students until all of them have mastered the sound. Finally in step g, individual students take turns saying the sound.

Teaching Techniques

You should hold the *Presentation Book* so that all the students can see the sound. Hold the book with one hand and point with the other hand. Use the following procedures to present the sound.

1. Touch the large ball of the arrow and say, "Your turn. Get ready."
2. Pause for one second.
3. Quickly move your finger to the second ball of the arrow. This movement acts as a signal for the students to say the sound.
4. Touch the second ball for two seconds. Because **mmm** is a continuous sound, the students say the sound for as long as you touch the second ball.

When presenting this task, make sure that you do not block the students' view of the letter. Always touch the balls, not the letter. Also, make sure your signal timing is consistent. Always pause for one second before moving to the second ball, and always point to the second ball for two seconds.

Step f requires you to repeat step e until all students are "firm." Students are "firm" when every one of them has mastered the sound. Every student must be able to say the sound for as long as you touch it.

In step g, you test individual students. You do not have to give an individual test to every student on every task. However, during the course of a lesson, every student should receive at least two or three individual tests. Try to give most individual tests to the slower students in the group, so that you can be sure that they have mastered each task.

Correcting Mistakes

To correct mistakes, use the specified correction procedure.

1. *Model* the correct answer by saying the sound.
2. *Lead* the students by saying the sound with them.
3. *Test* the students by having them say the sound by themselves.

In order to provide a *retest*, present the sound again at a later point in the lesson.

Practice Script 2

The following script appears in Lesson 27 of *Reading Mastery I*. The script introduces the sound **d**.

SOUNDS

TASK 2   Introducing the new sound d as in dad

---

a. Touch the ball of the arrow for **d**. We always have to say this sound fast. The little arrow under the sound tells me that I can't stop under this sound. My turn to say it fast. Slash to the end of the arrow as you say   d. Return to the ball. My turn to say it fast again. Slash to the end of the arrow as you say   d.
b. Touch the ball of the arrow. Your turn. Say it fast. Slash to the end of the arrow. d. Yes, d.
c. Repeat *b* until firm.
d. Call on different children to do *b*.

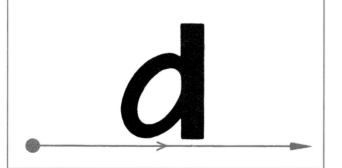

Description

This script is similar to Practice Script 1, except that the presentation has been streamlined and the correction procedure no longer appears. (Printed correction procedures are included only in the first few appearances of a task, but they can still be used to correct student errors on subsequent appearances of the task or on similar tasks.)

In step a, you model the correct way to say the sound. In step b, test the students by having them say the sound. In step c, you continue to test the students until all of them have mastered the sound. Finally in step d, individual students take turns saying the sound.

Teaching Techniques

Because **d** is a stop sound, you signal differently than for **mmm**.

1. Touch the large ball and say, "Your turn. Say it fast."
2. Pause for one second.
3. Slash your finger under the sound. The slash acts as a signal. When your finger passes under the sound, the students "say it fast."

Corrections

To correct mistakes, use the *model-lead-test-retest* procedure.

1. *Model* the correct answer by saying the sound.
2. *Lead* the students by saying the sound with them.
3. *Test* the students by having them say the sound by themselves.
4. *Retest* the students by presenting the sound again at a later point in the lesson.

Practice Script 3

The following script appears in Lesson 5 of *Reading Mastery II*. The script reviews sounds that the students have learned: **u** as in *under*, **ch** as in *chat*, **d** as in *mad*, **m** as in *ram* and so on.

TASK 1   **Sounds firm-up**

a. Point to the sounds.
   Get ready to tell me these sounds.
b. When I touch it, you say it.
   Keep on saying it as long as I touch it.
c. Point to each sound. Get ready.
   Touch the sound. *The children say the sound.*
   Lift your finger.

To correct
1. Immediately say the correct sound as you continue to touch it. Lift your finger.
2. Say it with me. Touch the sound and say it with children. Lift your finger.
3. Again. Repeat until firm.
4. All by yourselves. Get ready. Touch the sound. *The children say the sound.*

---

d. Repeat problem sounds until the children can correctly identify all sounds in order.

Individual test
Call on several children to identify one or more sounds.

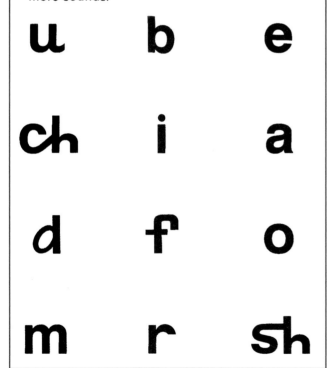

u b e

ch i a

d f o

m r sh

Description

In steps a–c, you test the students by having them say each sound. Step c also includes a correction procedure. In step d, you retest the students until you are sure that they have mastered each sound. Finally you administer individual tests.

Teaching Techniques

Your presentation is different than in the preceding scripts because there are no arrows under the sounds.

1. Point just below a sound, with your finger about an inch from the page.
2. Say, "Get ready."
3. Pause for one second.
4. Touch under the sound. Your touch acts as a signal. Always touch under the letter so that all the students can see the letter.

The students say the sound for as long as you touch under it. Touch continuous sounds, such as **u** and **m**, for two seconds; touch stop sounds, such as **ch**, **b** and **d**, for just an instant.

Corrections

To correct mistakes, use the specified correction procedure.

1. *Model* the correct answer by saying the sound.
2. *Lead* the students by saying the sound with them. (You may have to repeat this step several times.)
3. *Test* the students by having them say the sound by themselves.
4. *Retest* the students by proceeding to step d.

Practice Script 4

The following script appears in Lesson 46 of *Reading Mastery I*. The script introduces the word **meat.**

TASK 9 Children sound out the word and say it fast

a. Touch the first ball of the arrow for **mēat.** **Sound it out. Get ready.** Move quickly under each sound. *Mmmēēēt.*
b. Return to the first ball. **Again, sound it out. Get ready.** Move quickly under each sound. *Mmmēēēt.*
c. Repeat *b* until firm.
d. Return to the first ball. **Say it fast.** Slash. *Meat.* **Yes, what word?** *Meat.* **A hamburger is made of** (pause) **meat.**

Description

In steps a–c, the students sound out the word by saying each sound in sequence. Then, in step d, the students read the word normally by "saying it fast."

Teaching Techniques

To present the word, follow this procedure.

1. Touch the large ball and say, "Sound it out. Get ready."
2. Pause for one second.
3. Quickly move your finger to the second ball of the arrow. Hold your finger on the second ball for about one second, as the students say **mmm**.
4. Move your finger to the fourth ball and hold it there for just an instant, as the students say **t.**

Note that the small **a** does not have a ball under it. The students do not say any small silent letters; you simply move your finger past them.

After the students are proficient at sounding out the word, they "say it fast." Use the following procedure.

1. Touch the large ball of the arrow and say, "Say it fast."
2. Pause for one second.
3. Quickly slash under the word as the students "say it fast."

Corrections

Some students may have trouble "saying it fast." To correct mistakes, use a *model-test-retest* procedure.

1. *Model* the correct answer by sounding out the word and saying it fast.
2. *Test* the students by having them sound out the word and say it fast.
3. *Retest* the students by presenting the task again at a later point in the lesson.

Practice Script 5

The following script appears in Lesson 11 of *Reading Mastery II*.

TASK 10 **Read the fast way**

a. Read these words the fast way.
b. Touch the ball for **another.**
(Pause two seconds.) Get ready. (Signal.)
Another. Yes, **another.**
c. Repeat *b* for **whȳ, when,** and **funny.**

another

whȳ

when

funny

Description

This task reviews words that the students have already learned. The students read all the words "the fast way," without first sounding them out.

Teaching Techniques

To present the words, follow this procedure.

1. Touch the ball of the arrow.
2. Pause for two seconds. This pause gives the students time to examine the word.
3. Say, "Get ready."
4. Pause for one second.
5. Quickly slash under the word with your finger, as the students read the word.
6. Reinforce the students by repeating the word out loud.

Corrections

Correct mistakes by using a *process-test-retest* procedure.

1. Tell the students to use the sounding-out *process*, and direct them as they sound out the word.
2. *Test* the students by asking them, "What word?"
3. *Retest* the students by returning to the top of the column and presenting all of the words in order.

Practice Script 6

There are two basic procedures for presenting the Group Reading. The first procedure is used in *Reading Mastery I* and Lessons 1–80 of *Reading Mastery II*. The following script shows the first procedure. It appears in Lesson 14 of *Reading Mastery II*.

Description

In Task 12, the students read the title and the first part of the story aloud and in unison. In Task 13, the students take turns reading the rest of the story aloud. You call on different students to read one sentence each. Occasionally you direct the group to read a sentence in unison. In Task 14, the students take turns reading the story again as you present comprehension questions.

Teaching Techniques

Use the following procedure to conduct the reading.

1. Direct the students to touch under each word by saying, "First word," or "Next word."
2. Pause two seconds. This pause gives the students time to examine the word.
3. Say, "Get ready."
4. Pause for one second.
5. Clap your hands as the students read the word in unison.

The comprehension questions are cued by little numbers in your copy of the story. When the students read up to a number, you present the questions for that number. Sentences that contain numbers are always underlined. The students' version of the text does not contain any numbers or underlines.

The students should be looking at you when you present the questions, but they should continue to touch the current word in the story. For questions that require precise answers, you will need to use a **hand-drop signal**.

1. Hold out one hand as if you were stopping traffic.
2. Present the question.
3. Pause for one second.
4. Quickly drop your hand. Your hand-drop acts as a signal. If you want, you can also snap your fingers as you drop your hand.
5. Listen carefully to the students' answers and correct any mistakes.

Some comprehension questions do not require precise answers. You simply present these questions to the group and accept all reasonable answers.

Corrections

The students will make two basic types of mistakes during the Group Reading: word-identification errors and comprehension errors. To correct word-identification errors, follow the procedure specified in Task 14.

1. *Model* the correct answer by saying the word.
2. *Test* the student by having the student say the word.
3. *Retest* the student by having the student reread the sentence.

Comprehension errors tend to fall into two groups. For some questions, the students will give the right answer but they will say it incorrectly. For other questions the students will simply give the wrong answer.

When the students do not say the answer correctly, use the following procedure.

1. *Model* the correct answer by saying the answer correctly.
2. *Test* the students by having them say the word correctly.
3. *Retest* the students by repeating the question.

The corrections for wrong answers are a little more complicated. If the question is clearly answered by a sentence in the story, use the following procedure.

1. Demonstrate a *process* for answering the question by rereading the appropriate sentence.
2. *Test* the students by repeating the question.
3. *Retest* the student by repeating the question again at a later point in the lesson.

If the question is not clearly answered by a sentence in the story, use the following procedure.

1. *Model* the correct answer by saying the correct answer.
2. *Test* the students by having them say the correct answer.
3. *Test* the students again by repeating the question.
4. *Retest* the student by repeating the question again at a later point in the lesson.

TASK 12 First reading—title and three sentences

a. Everybody, open your reader to page 22.
b. Everybody, touch the title.
   Check to see that the children are touching under the first word of the title.
c. I'll clap and you read each word in the title the fast way. Don't sound it out. Just tell me the word.
d. First word. Check children's responses. (Pause two seconds.) Get ready. Clap. The children read *the.*
e. Next word. Check children's responses. (Pause two seconds.) Get ready. Clap. The children read *cow.*
f. Repeat e for the remaining words in the title.
g. Everybody, say the title. (Signal.)
   The cow boy and the cow.
   Yes, **the cow boy and the cow.**
h. Everybody, get ready to read this story the fast way.
i. First word. Check children's responses. (Pause two seconds.) Get ready. Clap. *A.*
j. Next word. Check children's responses. (Pause two seconds.) Get ready. Clap. *Cow boy.*
k. Repeat j for the remaining words in the first three sentences. Have the children reread the first three sentences until firm.

TASK 13 Remaining sentences

a. I'm going to call on different children to read a sentence. Everybody, follow along and point to the words. If you hear a mistake, raise your hand.
b. Call on a child. Read the next sentence.
c. Call on a different child. Read the next sentence.
d. Repeat c for most of the remaining sentences in the story.
e. Occasionally have the group read a sentence. When the group is to read, say:
   Everybody, read the next sentence.

(Pause two seconds.) Clap for each word in the sentence. Pause at least two seconds between claps.

TASK 14 Second reading—sentences and questions

a. You're going to read the story again. This time I'm going to ask questions.
b. Starting with the first word of the title. Check children's responses. Get ready. Clap as the children read the title.
c. Call on a child. Read the first sentence.

To correct word-identification errors (**from,** for example)
1. That word is **from.** What word? *From.*
2. Go back to the beginning of the sentence and read the sentence again.

---

d. Call on a different child. Read the next sentence.
e. Repeat d for most of the remaining sentences in the story.
f. Occasionally have the group read a sentence.
g. After each underlined sentence has been read, present each comprehension question specified below to the entire group.

[1] What's this story going to be about? (Signal.) *The cow boy and the cow.*
What do cow boys usually ride on? (Signal.) *Horses.*
[2] Why was this cow boy sad? (Signal.) *He did not have a horse.*
[3] What did the cow say? (Signal.) *But I can run as fast as a horse.*
[4] Do you think the cow can really jump better than a horse? *The children respond.* *We'll see.*
[5] Is the cow boy going to give the cow a try? (Signal.) *Yes.*
[6] Why did the other cow boys make fun of him? *The children respond.*
[7] Is this the end of the story? (Signal.) *No.* Next time we'll read more about the cow boy and the cow.

---

the cow boy and the cow[1]
   a cow boy was sad. hē did not havₑ a hŏrsₑ.[2] the other cow boys said, "hŏ, hŏ, that funny cow boy has nŏ hŏrsₑ."
   a cow cāmₑ up to the cow boy. the cow said, "if you arₑ a cow boy, you nēēd a cow. I am a cow."

   the cow boy said, "do not bē funny. cow boys do not rīdₑ on cows."
   the cow said, "but I can run as fast as a hŏrsₑ.[3] and I can jump better than a hŏrsₑ."[4]
   the cow boy said, "I will givₑ you a trȳ. but I will fēēl

very funny rīdiñg on a cow." sō the cow boy got on the cow.[5]
   then the other cow boys cāmₑ up the rōad. "hŏ, hŏ," they said. "look at that funny cow boy.[6] hē is trȳiñg to rīdₑ a cow."
   stop[7]

Practice Script 7

A second type of Group Reading procedure is used in Lessons 81–160 of *Reading Mastery II*. The following script for a comprehension passage is typical. It appears in Lesson 85 of *Reading Mastery II*.

Description

- Individual reading replaces group reading.
- Stories are presented in traditional textbook print.
- If the group makes no more than five errors by the time it reaches the five-error mark, you will reread the story to the children from the beginning to the five-error mark, stopping at the end of each underlined sentence to ask the specified comprehension questions.

Teaching Techniques

Children should follow along with their finger or a marker as you read. Encourage the children to look up when you ask a question but to "keep their place" with their finger or marker.

One of your major goals in reading the story to the children is to model inflection, appropriate responses to story content, *and* rate. Adjust your rate so that you read to them a little faster—but only a little faster—than you expect them to read on their individual checkouts. (That time is specified in the checkouts.) A good way to know if you're reading at an appropriate rate is to watch the children's fingers as they follow along. If their fingers are not in place, you're probably reading too fast. Never read to them as fast as you would if you were reading a story aloud during library time.

Corrections

The students will make two basic types of mistakes during the Group Reading: word-identification errors and comprehension errors. To correct word-identification errors, follow the same procedure specified in Script 6.

1. *Model* the correct word.
2. *Test* the student by having the student say the word.
3. *Retest* the student by having the student reread the sentence.

To correct comprehension errors when the students do not word the answer correctly, use the following procedure.

1. *Model* the correct answer.
2. *Test* by having the student say the answer correctly.
3. *Retest* the student by repeating the question.

To correct other comprehension errors, use the following procedure.

1. *Model* the correct answer by calling on another student to give the correct answer.
2. *Test* the student who gave an incorrect answer by repeating the question.
3. *Retest* the student by repeating the question at a later time in the lesson.

TASK 11 Reading—decoding

a. Everybody, look at the story on page 4.

b. Everybody, in the middle of the story there's a big red number 5 in a circle. Touch that number 5. **Check.** That 5 tells you that, if the group reads all the way to the 5 without making more than five errors, we can go on in the story. But if the group makes more than five errors, you have to go back and read the first part again. You have to keep reading it until you can read it without making more than five errors. I'll count the errors. I'll tell you about the big star later.

c. Everybody, touch the title of the story. Check.

d. I'm going to call on different children to read two or three sentences. Everybody, follow along. If you hear a mistake, raise your hand. Children who do not have their place lose their turn. Call on individual children to read two or three sentences. Do not ask comprehension questions.

To correct word-identification errors **(from,** for example)

1. That word is **from.** What word?
2. Go back to the beginning of the sentence and read the sentence again.
3. Tally all errors.

e. If the children make more than five errors: when they reach the 5, say, You made too many errors. Go back to the beginning of the story and we'll try again. Try to read more carefully this time. Call on individual children to read two or three sentences. Do not ask comprehension questions. Repeat step e until firm, and then go on to step f.

did don mope after he became a super man?[5]

don was hopping around the store in his cap and his cape. he was hitting the walls and making holes. he was having a lot of fun.

all at once he stopped. he said, "I will go outside and show what a super man I am."[6]

When don left the store, he didn't open the door. he ran into the door. "Crash."[7]

Some boys were standing outside the store. They said, "look at that funny man in a cap and a cape."

★ don said, "I am no funny man. I am a super man."

don ran to a car that was parked near the store.[8] he picked the car up and gave it a big heave.[9] The car crashed into another car. ⑤

The boys yelled, "let's get out of here. That man is a nut."

"Come back," don shouted. "let me show you how super I am."

but the boys did not come back. They ran as fast as they could go.[10]

don said, "I think I will fly to the top of this store." So he did.[11] Then he said, "I think I will dive down to the street." So he did. he took a dive. "Crash." he made a big hole in the street.[12]

"This is a lot of fun," don said.[13]

To be continued[14]

f. When the children read to the number 5 without making more than five errors: say, Good reading. I'll read the story from the beginning to the 5 and ask you some questions. Read the story, starting with the title. Stop at the end of each underlined sentence and ask the specified question. When you reach the 5, call on individual children to continue reading the story. Have each child read two or three sentences. Ask the specified questions at the end of each underlined sentence.

[1] What's Don going to do in this story? (Signal.) *Have super fun.*

[2] Everybody, say that question. (Signal.) *Who gave Don the dime?* What's the answer? (Signal.) *The woman.*

[3] What's the answer? (Signal.) *To his arm.*

[4] Say that question. (Signal.) *Was he doing good things?* What's the answer? (Signal.) *No.*

[5] What's the answer? (Signal.) *No.*

[6] What's he going to do? (Signal.) *Go outside and show what a super man he is.*

[7] What went crash? (Signal.) *The door.* Why? *The children respond.*

[8] What do you think he'll do to that car? *The children respond.* Let's find out.

[9] What did he do to the car? *The children respond.*

[10] Who ran? (Signal.) *The boys.* Why did they run? *The children respond.* I don't blame them. I'd run away, too.

[11] What did he do? (Signal.) *Fly to the top of the store.*

[12] How did the hole get in the street? *The children respond.*

[13] What did he say? (Signal.) *This is a lot of fun.*

[14] Will there be more Don stories? (Signal.) *Yes.*

Practice Script 8

Throughout Levels 3 through 6, students read selections within an error limit and answer comprehension questions.

The following script for a story comprehension passage is typical of the Group Reading procedure. It appears in Lesson 6 of *Reading Mastery* Level 5.

Description

Individual students take turns reading the passage aloud. After students complete each section, ask the questions for that section.

For questions that require precise answers, the answers are preceded by the word "Response." For questions that do not require precise answers, the answers are preceded by the word "Idea."

Teaching Techniques

In this practice script, all of the questions are presented to individual students, and no signal is required. However, in some Group Reading scripts, certain questions are presented to the entire group. Use a hand-drop signal for these questions. (The hand-drop signal is discussed in Practice Script 6.)

Corrections

The students will make two basic types of mistakes during the Group Reading: word-identification errors and comprehension errors. To correct word-identification errors, use the following procedure.

1. *Model* the correct word.
2. *Test* the student by having the student say the word.
3. *Retest* the student by having the student reread the sentence.

To correct comprehension errors, use the following procedure.

1. *Model* the correct answer by calling on another student to give the correct answer.
2. *Test* the student who gave the incorrect answer by repeating the question.
3. *Retest* the student by repeating the question at a later time in the lesson.

READING ALOUD

1. The error limit for this chapter is six.
2. (Call on individual students to read two or three sentences each.)
3. (After students complete each section, ask the questions for that section.)

There was no attic at all and no cellar—except a small hole, dug in the ground, called a cyclone cellar. The family could go into the cellar in case one of those great whirlwinds arose, mighty enough to crush any building in its path. The cellar was reached by a trapdoor in the middle of the floor. A ladder inside led down into a small, dark hole.

When Dorothy stood in the doorway and looked outside, she could see nothing but the great, gray prairie on every side. No trees or houses could be seen on the flat country that reached the edge of the sky in all directions.

- What is the "great whirlwind"? (Idea: *A cyclone.*)
- What was the hole under the floor called? (Response: *A cyclone cellar.*)
- What did they use the cyclone cellar for? (Idea: *To hide from cyclones.*)
- How would you climb down into the cellar after you opened the trapdoor? (Idea: *On a ladder.*)
- Everybody, look at the picture. The picture shows what you have just been reading about. The horizon is the line where the land meets the sky. Run your finger along the horizon. ✓
- What is the funny cloud on the left side of the picture? (Response: *A cyclone.*)
- Who is standing in the doorway of the house? (Idea: *Dorothy.*)
- What people are standing in the field? (Idea: *Uncle Henry and Aunt Em.*)

The sun had baked the plowed land into a gray mass with little cracks running through it. Not even the grass was green, for the sun had burned the tops of the grass blades until they were the same gray color as the land. Once, the house had been painted white, but the sun blistered the paint and the rains washed it away, and now the house was as dull and gray as everything else.

When Aunt Em came here to live, she was young and pretty. The sun and wind had changed her, too. They had taken the sparkle from her eyes and left them a sober gray. They had taken the red from her cheeks and lips, and they were gray also. She was thin and she never smiled, now. ♦

- What color is the house now? (Response: *Gray.*)
- Had the house always been gray? (Response: *No.*)
- Name two things that made the house's color change. (Ideas: *The sun blistered the paint; the rain washed the paint away.*)
- What other things in the story are gray? (Ideas: *Prairie; grass; land; Aunt Em.*)
- Had Aunt Em's eyes, cheeks, and lips always been gray? (Response: *No.*)
- What made Aunt Em change? (Ideas: *The sun and wind; her hard life.*)

Practice Script 9

Beginning in *Reading Mastery* Levels 3–6, the word lists are printed in the students' books. You present vocabulary information about specific words that the students read.

The *Presentation Books* contain presentation scripts for the word lists as well as reproductions of the student material.

The following vocabulary exercise appears in Lesson 34 of *Reading Mastery* Level 3.

1
1. neither
2. remind
3. manage
4. prove

EXERCISE 2

READING WORDS

Column 1

a. **Find lesson 34 in your textbook.** ✓
- Touch column 1. ✓
- (Teacher reference:)

1. **neither**	3. **manage**
2. **remind**	4. **prove**

b. Word 1 is **neither.** What word? (Signal.) *Neither.*
- Spell **neither.** Get ready. (Tap for each letter.) *N-E-I-T-H-E-R.*
c. Word 2 is **remind.** What word? (Signal.) *Remind.*
- Spell **remind.** Get ready. (Tap for each letter.) *R-E-M-I-N-D.*
d. Word 3 is **manage.** What word? (Signal.) *Manage.*
- Spell **manage.** Get ready. (Tap for each letter.) *M-A-N-A-G-E.*
- When you work hard to do something, you manage to do it. Here's another way of saying **He worked hard to keep swimming: He managed to keep swimming.**

- Your turn. What's another way of saying **He worked hard to keep swimming?** (Signal.) *He managed to keep swimming.*
- What's another way of saying **The baby worked hard to walk?** (Signal.) *The baby managed to walk.*
e. Word 4 is **prove.** What word? (Signal.) *Prove.*
- Spell **prove.** Get ready. (Tap for each letter.) *P-R-O-V-E.*
- When you prove something, you show that it is true. When you prove that you can stand up, you show it's true that you can stand up.
- What would you have to do to prove that they are serving spaghetti for lunch? (Call on a student. Idea: *Show it's true that they are serving spaghetti for lunch.*)
- What would you have to do to prove that it is raining outside? (Call on a student. Idea: *Show it's true that it's raining outside.*)
f. Let's read those words again, the fast way.
- Word 1. What word? (Signal.) *Neither.*
- (Repeat for words 2–4.)
g. (Repeat step f until firm.)

Description

In steps a–e, you direct the students as they read and spell the four vocabulary words. In steps d and e, you also teach the meaning of two of these words. In step d, you *model* how to use the word in context and then *test* by asking the students to use it in a different context. In step e, you give the meaning of the word and then call on a student to paraphrase a sentence containing the new word.

Teaching Techniques

When presenting the word list, you will use audible signaling. Listen carefully as the students spell the word. Give a series of auditory signals—one for each letter. You must give auditory signals such as taps, claps, or finger snaps because the students are looking at their books and not at you.

When presenting the word meanings, you will either call on the group or call on individual students. When the group is tested in step d, the students must answer in unison. When you call on individual students in step e, answers may vary. Accept sentences that express the correct meaning. Rephrase by referring to the sentence in the script. "Yes, you show it's true that they are serving spaghetti for lunch."

Corrections

Some students may have trouble using the vocabulary words in context. For example, in step d they may say, *He worked hard to keep swimming*, instead of, *He managed to keep swimming*. Use a *model-test-retest* procedure to correct mistakes.

1. *Model* the correct word.
2. *Test* the students by having the group repeat the word.
3. *Test* the group again by repeating the question.
4. *Retest* the student by repeating the question at a later point in the lesson.

Practice Script 10

In certain lessons, you direct the students as they read skill exercises that appear in their textbooks (Levels 3–6). The following script appears in Lesson 49 of *Reading Mastery* Level 6.

Description

The students take turns reading parts of the exercise aloud. After they complete each section, you present the questions specified in the *Presentation Book*. These questions are always presented to individual students.

EXERCISE 3

METAPHORS

1. Everybody, turn to part D at the end of today's story. ✓
- (Call on individual students to read several sentences each.)
- (At the end of each section, present the questions for that section.)

Write the answers for items 1–6.
   A metaphor is like a simile except it doesn't use the word *like*.

- Name the kind of figurative language that is like a simile. (Response: *Metaphor.*)
- How is a metaphor different from a simile? (Idea: *It doesn't use the word like.*)

   Here's an accurate statement: *The woman was very smart.* Here's a metaphor: *The woman was a walking encyclopedia.*
1. What two things are the same in that metaphor?

- What's the answer? (Response: *The woman, an encyclopedia.*)

2. How could they be the same?

- What's the answer? (Idea: *Both are full of information.*)

   Here's another metaphor: *The man was a rattlesnake.*
3. What two things are the same in that metaphor?

- What's the answer? (Response: *The man, a rattlesnake.*)

4. How could they be the same?

- What's the answer? (Ideas: *Both are dangerous.*)
- You'll write the answers to the items later.

D METAPHORS

Write the answers for items 1–6.

A metaphor is like a simile except it doesn't use the word *like*.

Here's an accurate statement: *The woman was very smart*. Here's a metaphor: *The woman was a walking encyclopedia*.

1. What two things are the same in that metaphor?
2. How could they be the same?

Here's another metaphor: *The man was a rattlesnake*.

3. What two things are the same in that metaphor?
4. How could they be the same?

Here's another metaphor: *Miss Minchin was a jailer*.

5. What two things are the same in that metaphor?
6. How could they be the same?

Teaching Techniques

Because all the questions are presented to individual students, no signals are used. Call on a different student to answer each question. Lower-performing students should be called on more frequently so you can be sure they have mastered the skill.

Corrections

Use a *model-test-retest* procedure to correct mistakes.

1. *Model* by calling on another student to give the correct answer.
2. *Test* the student who made a mistake by repeating the question.
3. *Retest* the student by repeating the question at a later time in the lesson.

Scope and Sequence

The following scope-and-sequence chart provides an overview of the skills taught in the *Reading Mastery* Classic series. The skills are divided into four principal areas: decoding skills, comprehension skills, literary skills, and study skills.

Decoding Skills

Reading Mastery uses a widely acclaimed phonics method that features step-by-step instruction for all decoding skills.

Decoding Readiness: Students learn blending, sequencing, and matching skills that prepare them for decoding.

Sounds and Letters: Students learn letter sounds in a carefully programmed sequence. New letters are introduced every few lessons and then systematically reviewed.

Words: Students learn how to sound out and read regularly spelled words and how to read irregularly spelled words.

Sentences and Stories: Students learn how to read sentences, and then entire stories. Individual checkouts monitor reading rate and accuracy.

Comprehension Skills

Reading Mastery provides thorough instruction in reading comprehension. Oral questions, written questions, and skill exercises develop comprehension in five important areas.

Comprehension Readiness: Students learn how to follow directions and how to answer questions about pictures.

Vocabulary: Students learn how to identify word meanings and how to interpret definitions.

Literal Comprehension: Students learn how to understand the explicit meaning of a text.

Interpretive Comprehension: Students learn how to interpret the implicit meaning of a text.

Reasoning: Students learn how to analyze the underlying logic of a text.

Literary Skills

Reading Mastery stresses literary appreciation and interpretation. Students read a wide range of literature and carefully analyze content and style.

Characters and Settings: Students learn how to interpret complex characters and settings.

Literary Devices: Students learn how to interpret figurative language and other elements of literary style.

Types of Literature: Students learn about various types of literature and read examples of each type.

Study Skills

Reading Mastery teaches the writing and reference skills that are necessary for effective studying.

Writing: Students gradually develop writing skills, first by copying words and stories, then by writing answers to questions, and finally by writing whole paragraphs, stories, and poems.

Reference Materials: Students learn how to interpret a wide variety of reference materials, such as maps, diagrams, time lines, and graphs.

Decoding Skills

	I	II	FC	3	4	5	6
Decoding Readiness							
Pronouncing individual sounds	◆		◆				
Sequencing from left to right	◆		◆				
Blending sounds orally	◆		◆				
Identifying rhyming sounds	◆		◆				
Sounds and Letters							
Reading short vowels	◆	◆	◆				
Reading long vowels	◆	◆	◆				
Reading voiced consonants	◆	◆	◆				
Reading unvoiced consonants	◆	◆	◆				
Reading sound combinations	◆	◆	◆	◆			
Identifying vowel names		◆	◆				
Identifying consonant names		◆	◆				
Identifying alphabetical order		◆	◆	◆			
Words							
Reading regularly spelled words	◆	◆	◆	◆	◆	◆	◆
Reading irregularly spelled words	◆	◆	◆	◆	◆	◆	◆
Recognizing rhyming words	◆		◆	◆		◆	◆
Recognizing inflected endings	◆		◆		◆	◆	
Recognizing compound words		◆	◆	◆	◆	◆	
Reading word lists for accuracy		◆	◆	◆	◆	◆	
Spelling difficult words		◆	◆	◆	◆		
Sentences and Stories							
Reading aloud	◆	◆	◆	◆	◆	◆	◆
Reading silently	◆	◆	◆	◆	◆	◆	◆
Reading aloud for rate and accuracy	◆	◆	◆	◆	◆	◆	
Identifying punctuation marks	◆		◆		◆	◆	

Comprehension Skills

	I	II	FC	3	4	5	6
Comprehension Readiness							
Following oral directions	◆	◆	◆	◆	◆	◆	◆
Answering questions about pictures	◆	◆	◆	◆	◆	◆	◆
Associating pictures with words	◆		◆				
Drawing pictures based on a story	◆		◆				
Repeating sentences	◆		◆	◆	◆		
Vocabulary							
Identifying the meanings of common words	◆	◆	◆	◆	◆	◆	◆
Writing the names of pictured objects	◆	◆	◆				
Comprehending vocabulary definitions				◆	◆	◆	◆
Using vocabulary words in context				◆	◆	◆	◆
Identifying homonyms and homographs				◆		◆	
Comprehending contractions				◆			
Using context to predict word meaning						◆	◆
Literal Comprehension							
Answering literal questions about a text	◆	◆	◆	◆	◆	◆	◆
Identifying literal cause and effect	◆	◆	◆	◆	◆	◆	◆
Recalling details and events	◆	◆	◆	◆	◆	◆	◆
Following written directions	◆	◆	◆	◆	◆	◆	◆
Memorizing facts and rules		◆	◆	◆	◆		
Sequencing narrative events				◆	◆	◆	◆
Interpretive Comprehension							
Predicting narrative outcomes	◆	◆	◆	◆	◆	◆	◆
Relating titles to story content	◆	◆	◆	◆	◆	◆	
Inferring causes and effects		◆	◆	◆	◆	◆	◆
Inferring story details and events		◆	◆	◆	◆	◆	◆
Making comparisons				◆	◆	◆	◆
Inferring details relevant to a main idea					◆	◆	◆
Inferring the main idea				◆		◆	◆
Outlining						◆	◆
Inferring story morals				◆		◆	
Reasoning							
Using rules to classify objects		◆	◆	◆	◆		
Completing written deductions		◆	◆	◆			◆
Drawing conclusions				◆	◆	◆	◆
Using rules to predict outcomes				◆	◆		
Evaluating problems and solutions					◆	◆	◆
Identifying relevant evidence					◆		◆
Identifying contradictions							◆
Identifying inferential questions							◆
Identifying logical fallacies							◆

Literary Skills

	I	II	FC	3	4	5	6
Character and Settings							
Interpreting a character's feelings	◆	◆	◆	◆	◆	◆	◆
Pretending to be a character	◆	◆	◆	◆	◆	◆	◆
Interpreting a character's motives		◆	◆	◆	◆	◆	◆
Inferring a character's point of view	◆	◆	◆	◆	◆	◆	◆
Predicting a character's actions				◆	◆	◆	◆
Identifying features of a setting				◆	◆	◆	◆
Identifying a character's traits				◆	◆	◆	◆
Literary Devices							
Interpreting figurative language							◆
Interpreting extended dialogues							◆
Interpreting substitute words							◆
Interpreting shortened sentences							◆
Interpreting combined sentences						◆	◆
Interpreting literary irony							◆
Types of Literature							
Reading realistic fiction	◆	◆	◆	◆	◆	◆	◆
Reading fantasy	◆	◆	◆	◆	◆	◆	◆
Reading factual articles		◆	◆	◆	◆	◆	◆
Distinguishing between realism and fantasy				◆		◆	
Distinguishing between fact and fiction					◆	◆	
Reading biographies						◆	◆
Reading poetry				◆	◆	◆	◆
Reading drama				◆	◆		◆

Study Skills

	I	II	FC	3	4	5	6
Writing							
Copying letters	◆	◆	◆				
Copying words	◆		◆				
Copying sentences	◆	◆	◆				
Writing answers to questions		◆	◆	◆	◆	◆	◆
Organizing information					◆	◆	◆
Completing writing assignments				◆	◆	◆	◆
Reference Materials							
Interpreting maps				◆	◆	◆	◆
Interpreting standard measurements				◆	◆		
Interpreting diagrams				◆	◆	◆	◆
Interpreting time lines				◆	◆	◆	
Filling out forms				◆			◆
Using reference sources				◆	◆	◆	◆
Interpreting glossaries				◆	◆	◆	
Interpreting indexes				◆	◆	◆	
Interpreting graphs				◆	◆		◆

Placement Tests

The six placement tests can be used to determine the level of *Reading Mastery* Classic Edition in which your students should be placed. There is a separate test for each level. The placement test for *Reading Mastery I* can be used to determine if students should be placed in *Fast Cycle*.

Ideally, placement testing should be conducted at the beginning of the school year. Begin placement testing by giving students in grades 1–6 the placement test that corresponds with their grade level. Give the placement test for Level I to kindergarten children.

The following sections give specific instructions for each placement test.

Reading Mastery I

The placement test for *Reading Mastery I* is administered to individual students in turn. You present test items aloud and tally the student's correct answers on a score sheet. You should administer the test in a place that is somewhat removed from the other students, so that they will not overhear the testing.

The test items use several typefaces.

- This red type indicates what you say.
- This light type indicates what you do.
- *This italic type shows the student's answers.*

Some test items require you to point to large letters that appear in this book. For these items, hold the book so that the child can see the letters.

The score sheet appears in the next column. Make one copy of the score sheet for each student. To use the score sheet, simply circle 1 point or 2 points if the student answers correctly.

Student's Name _____

Date _____

SCORE SHEET - *Reading Mastery I*

PART 1		PART 2	
Item	**Points**	**Item**	**Points**
1b	0 1	1a	0 2
1c	0 1	1b	0 2
2b	0 1	2b	0 1
	0 1		0 1
	0 1	2c	0 1
	0 1		0 1
	0 1	2d	0 1
2d	0 1		0 1
	0 1	*Subtotal*	☐
	0 1		
	0 1		
	0 1		
3b	0 2		
3c	0 2		
4b	0 2		
4d	0 2		
Subtotal	☐	*Total*	☐

PLACEMENT TEST

PART 1

Task 1   Total possible: 2 points

(Circle 1 point on the scoring sheet for each correct response at *b* and *c*.)

This is an oral task. For step *c*, say the sound **d**, not the letter name.

a. You're going to say some sounds.
b. (test item) Say   (pause) **rrr.**   *rrr.*
c. (test item) Now say   (pause) **d.**   *d.*

Task 2   Total possible: 10 points

(Circle 1 point on the scoring sheet for each correct response at *b*.)

a. Point to the sounds. These are sounds.
Point to the boxed **m**. This sound is   (pause)
mmm. What sound?   Touch **m.** *mmm.*
b. (test items) Point to each unboxed sound in the column. For each sound, ask: Is this (pause) **mmm?**

(Circle 1 point on the scoring sheet for each correct response at step *d*.)

c. Point to the boxed **a.** This sound is   (pause)
ăăă. What sound?   Touch **a.** *ăăă.*
d. (test items) Point to each unboxed sound in the column. For each sound, ask: Is this (pause) **ăăă?**

m

a

m

a

m

a

PLACEMENT TEST

Task 3 Total possible: 4 points

(Circle 2 points on the scoring sheet for each correct response at *b* and *c*.)

a. Let's play Say It Fast. Listen. **Ice** (pause) **box.** I can say it fast. **Icebox.**
b. **(test item)** Listen. **Foot** (pause) **ball.** (Pause.) Say it fast. *Football.* Yes, **football.**
c. **(test item)** Here's another word. Listen. (Pause.) **Nnnōōōzzz.** (Pause.) Say it fast. *Nose.* Yes, **nose.**

Task 4 Total possible: 4 points

(Circle 2 points on the scoring sheet for each correct response at *b* and *d*.)

This is an oral task. Do not stop between the sounds when saying zzzoooo or wwwēēē.

a. First I'll say a word slowly. Then you'll say that word slowly. I'll say (pause) **zoo** slowly. Listen. (Pause.) **Zzzoooo.**
b. **(test item)** Your turn. Say (pause) **zzzoooo.** *Zzzoooo.*
   (A child scores 2 points if he or she says the correct sounds without stopping between the sounds.)
c. Now I'll say (pause) **wē** slowly. Listen. (Pause.) **Wwwēēē.**
d. **(test item)** Your turn. Say (pause) **wwwēēē.**
   (A child scores 2 points if he or she says the correct sounds without stopping between the sounds.)

> Add the number of points the child earned on part 1. Note: Administer part 2 **only** to children who made 19 or 20 points on part 1.

PART 2

Task 1 Total possible: 4 points

(Circle 2 points on the scoring sheet for each correct response at *a* and *b*.)

a. **(test item)** Point to the boxed **m.** Let's see if you remember this sound. (Pause.) What sound? Touch **m.** *mmm.*
b. **(test item)** Point to the boxed **a.** Let's see if you remember this sound. (Pause.) What sound? Touch **a.** *ăăă.*

Task 2 Total possible: 6 points

(Circle 1 point on the scoring sheet for each correct response at *b*, *c*, and *d*.)

a. I'll say a word slowly. Then I'll say it fast. Listen. (Pause.) **Mmmaaannn.** (Pause.) I can say it fast. **Man.**
b. **(test item)** Your turn. Say (pause) **iiinnn.** *iiinnn.*
   (test item) Say it fast. *In.*
c. **(test item)** Your turn. Say (pause) **aaat.** *Aaat.*
   (test item) Say it fast. *At.*
d. **(test item)** Your turn. Say (pause) **sssiiit.** *Sssiiit.*
   (test item) Say it fast. *Sit.*

End of Placement Test

Placement Guidelines

Part 1 of the Placement Test

Children who made 0–14 points begin with *Reading Mastery I*, Lesson 1.

Children who made 15–18 points begin with *Reading Mastery I*, Lesson 11.

Children who made 19–20 points should proceed with Part 2 of the placement test.

Part 2 of the Placement Test

Children who made 0–7 points begin with *Reading Mastery I*, Lesson 11.

Children who made 8–10 points should be placed, if possible, in *Reading Mastery: Fast Cycle I.*

Reading Mastery II

For the *Reading Mastery II* placement test, each student reads a story aloud as you count the student's decoding errors.

You will need to make one copy of the story on page 71. You should administer the test in a place that is somewhat removed from the other students, so that they will not overhear the testing.

Use the following procedures to administer the placement test.

1. Give the student a copy of the story.
2. Point to the passage and say, "I want you to read the story out loud. Take your time. Start with the title and read the story as well as you can."
3. Time the student and make one tally mark for each error. Use the following guidelines when tallying errors.
   - If the student misreads a word, tell the student the word and mark one error.
   - If the student reads a word incorrectly and then correctly, mark one error.
   - If the student sounds out a word instead of reading it normally, mark one error. (Note: Correct the student the first time the student sounds out a word. Ask the student, "What word is that?" If the student reads the word correctly, do not mark an error. If the student sounds out the word, mark an error. Do not correct the student on any subsequent sounding-outs.)
   - If the student does not identify a word within four seconds, tell the student the word and mark one error.
   - If the student skips a word, point to the word. If the student does not read the word correctly, mark one error.
   - If the student skips a line, point to the line. If the student does not read the line correctly, mark one error.
4. After two and a half minutes, stop the student. Count every word not read as an error. For example, if the student is eight words from the end of the passage at the end of the time limit, count eight errors.
5. Total the student's errors.

Placement Guidelines

Place your students as follows:

- Students who made 0 to 3 errors should be placed in Lesson 11 of *Reading Mastery II*.
- Students who made 4 to 8 errors should be placed in Lesson 1 of *Reading Mastery II*.
- Students who made more than 8 errors should be placed in *Reading Mastery I*. To determine an appropriate placement for these students, give them the individual rate-and-accuracy checkouts from *Reading Mastery I*. Start with the checkout for Lesson 140. If the student passes this checkout, place the student in Lesson 141. If the student does not pass this checkout, present the checkout for Lesson 130. Continue working backward until the student passes a checkout. Place the student in the lesson that follows the checkout lesson.

the cow on the rōₐd

lots of men went down the
rōₐd in a littlₑ car.

a cow was sittīng on the
rōₐd. sō the men ran to the cow.
"wē will lift this cow," they said.

but the men did not lift the
cow. "this cow is sō fat wē can
not lift it."

the cow said, "I am not sō
fat. I can lift mē." then the cow
got in the car.

the men said, "now wē can
not get in the car." sō the men
sat on the rōₐd and the cow
went hōmₑ in the car.

the end

Reading Mastery II Placement Test

Guidelines for Placement Tests, Levels 3, 4, 5, and 6

The placement tests for *Reading Mastery* Levels 3, 4, 5, and 6 are similar in many respects. In part 1 of each test, individual students read a passage aloud as you count decoding errors. You will need to make one copy of the appropriate test for each student and mark that copy. You should administer Part 1 in a place that is somewhat removed from the other students, so that they will not overhear the testing.

How to Count Decoding Errors

Use the following guidelines when counting decoding errors on Part 1.

- If the student misreads a word, count one error.
- If the student omits a word ending, such as *s* or *ed*, count one error.

- If the student reads a word incorrectly and then correctly, count one error.
- If the student sounds out a word instead of reading it normally, count one error.
- If the student does not identify a word within three seconds, tell the student the word and count one error.
- If the student skips a word, count one error.
- If the student skips a line, point to the line and count one error.
- If the student does not finish the passage within the given time limit, count every word not read as an error. For example, if the student is eight words from the end of the passage at the end of the time limit, count eight errors.

Reading Mastery Level 3

Level 3 Placement Test Directions

Instructions for Part 1

Reproduce the Placement Test that appears on page 74. Make one copy for each student that you are to test. Then follow these steps:

1. Call a student to a corner of the room, where the test will be given.

2. Show a blank copy of the test to the student. Use the student's copy of the placement test to mark errors.

Part 1 Vocabulary Reading

- (Teacher reference:)

1. expert	7. difference
2. clinic	8. mirror
3. interest	9. through
4. changes	10. practicing
5. themselves	11. questions
6. people	

3. Point to the column of words at the top of the test. Tell the student: Touch word 1. (Wait.) That word is **expert.**

4. Repeat step 3 for words 2–11.

5. Your turn to read those words.

6. Word 1. What word?

7. Repeat step 6 for words 2–11.

Part 1 Passage Reading

8. Point to the passage in Part 1.

9. Tell the student: You're going to read this passage out loud. I want you to read it as well as you can. Don't try to read it so fast that you make mistakes. But don't read it so slowly that it doesn't make any sense. You have two minutes to read the passage. Go.

10. Time the student. If the student takes more than three seconds on a word, say the word, count it as an error, and permit the student to continue reading. To record errors, make one tally mark for each error.

Use the guidelines detailed above when counting decoding errors in Part 1.

Remember to count each word not read by the end of the two-minute time limit as an error. For example, if the student is eight words from the end of the passage by the end of the time limit, count eight errors.

11. Collect the test sheet.

Instructions for Part 2

After you've administered Part 1 to all the students, present Part 2, which is a group test. Administer Part 2 no more than 2 hours after students complete Part 1. Here are the steps to follow:

1. Assemble the students.

2. Give each student a copy of the placement test.

3. Give the group these instructions: At the bottom of the page are questions about the passage that you read earlier. Write the answers. You have two minutes to finish.

4. Time the students. Collect the test sheets after two minutes.

Answer Key for Part 2

1. What was the first name of the man in the story? _____ Bill

2. Underline 4 things he did to try to be more interesting.
   - frown more
   - smile more
   - whisper
   - ask questions
   - answer questions
   - talk louder
   - talk softer
   - talk faster
   - talk slower

3. His problem was that he
   - was old
   - had five dogs
   - put people to sleep

4. He practiced in front of
   - his wife
   - the mirror
   - the TV

5. Who came over when he was practicing?
   - a sleeper
   - a dog expert
   - a sleep expert

6. Name the place where she worked.
   _____ Sleep More Clinic

Placement Guidelines

Use the table below to determine placement for each student.

Errors	Placement
If a student makes 7 errors or more on Part 1 **OR** 2 errors or more on Part 2	Place the student in a reading program more elementary than *Reading Mastery* Level 3, possibly *Reading Mastery* Level I or Level II.
If a student makes no more than 6 errors on Part 1 **AND** no more than 1 error on Part 2	Place the student at *Reading Mastery* Level 3, Lesson 1.

PLACEMENT TEST

Part 1

Bill tried to say things that would interest other people. He asked questions and tried to get people to talk about themselves. He said things that were funny. He talked faster and louder. He tried to smile more when he talked. But all those changes made no difference. After Bill was through speaking, everybody else was sleeping.

One day, Bill was at home. He was practicing in front of the mirror. He smiled, moved around a lot, and talked to the mirror.

Just then the door bell rang. Bill opened the door and saw a woman who said, "I am an expert at making people sleep. I work for the Sleep More Clinic. We help people who have trouble sleeping. I hear that you can make people sleep, too."

"Yes," Bill said. "If I speak for a while, people will sleep."

"That is interesting," the sleep expert said. "Can you explain why people sleep?"

"Yes, I can," Bill said.

1. expert
2. clinic
3. interest
4. changes
5. themselves
6. people
7. difference
8. mirror
9. through
10. practicing
11. questions

Part 2

1. What was the first name of the man in the story?

   _____

2. Underline 4 things he did to try to be more interesting.

   • frown more   • talk louder
   • smile more   • talk softer
   • whisper   • talk faster
   • ask questions   • talk slower
   • answer questions

3. His problem was that he

   • was old • had five dogs • put people to sleep

4. He practiced in front of

   • his wife • the mirror • the TV

5. Who came over when he was practicing?

   • a sleeper • a dog expert • a sleep expert

6. Name the place where she worked.

   _____

Reading Mastery Level 4

Level 4 Placement Test Directions

Instructions for Part 1

Reproduce the one-page Placement Test that appears on page 76. Make one copy for each student that you are to test.

1. Call a student to a corner of the room, where the test will be given.

2. Give a copy of the test to the student.

3. Point to the column of words at the top of the test. Tell the student: "Touch word 1." (Wait.) "That word is California."

4. Repeat step 3 for words 2–5.

5. Point to the passage on part 1.

6. Tell the student: "You're going to read this passage out loud. I want you to read it as well as you can. Don't try to read it so fast that you make mistakes. But don't read it so slowly that it doesn't make any sense. You have two minutes to read the passage. Go."

7. Time the student. If the student takes more than three seconds on a word, say the word, count it as an error, and permit the student to continue reading. To record errors, make one tally mark for each error.

Count all the following behaviors as errors:

- Misreading a word (Count as one error.)

- Omitting a word part (Listen carefully for *s* and *ed*.) (Count as one error.)

- Sounding out a word but not saying the word at a normal speaking rate (Count as one error.)

- Skipping a word (Count as one error.)

- Skipping a line (Immediately show the student the correct line.) (Count as one error.)

- Not identifying a word within three seconds (Tell the word.) (Count as one error.)

- Reading a word incorrectly and then reading it correctly (Count as one error.)

Also count each word not read by the end of the two-minute time limit as an error. For example, if the student is eight words from the end of the passage by the end of the time limit, count eight errors.

Instructions for Part 2

After you've administered Part 1 to all the students, present Part 2 to those students who made no more than six errors on Part 1. (Part 2 is a group test.)

1. Assemble the students.

2. Give each student a copy of the placement test.

3. Make sure the students have pencils.

4. Give the group these instructions: "These are questions about the passage that you read earlier. Write the answers to the comprehension items at the bottom of your paper. You have five minutes to finish the questions."

5. Collect the test sheets after five minutes.

Answer Key for Part 2

1. *Idea:* Because the ship was on fire
2. Linda, Kathy   3. lifeboats
4. Linda   5. 13   6. 10   7. hand
8. Idea: In a lifeboat   9. Japan
10. Idea: To see their father   11. 3 days

PLACEMENT TEST

Part 1

"Fire! Fire!" a voice said over the loudspeaker. "The forward deck is on fire," the voice announced. "Everybody, leave the ship. Get into the lifeboats!"

Linda and her sister were on their way from the United States to Japan. Linda was thirteen years old, three years older than Kathy. Their father was in Japan, and they were on their way to visit him. Three days before, they had left California on a great ship called an ocean liner. They were now somewhere in the middle of the Pacific Ocean.

"Fire! Fire!" the voice shouted. "Everybody get into the lifeboats!"

People were running this way and that way on the deck of the ship. They were yelling and crying.

"Hold on to my hand," Linda said. The girls went to the lifeboats. People were all around them, shoving and yelling. Linda could not see much. She was afraid. Suddenly she was no longer holding Kathy's hand.

Suddenly a strong pair of arms grabbed Linda. "In you go," a voice said. A big man picked Linda up and put her in the lifeboat.

"Where's my sister?" Linda asked. Linda looked but she couldn't see her younger sister.

1. California
2. Pacific
3. lifeboat
4. Japan
5. loudspeaker

Part 2

1. Why was everybody trying to leave the ship?
_____

2. Name the two sisters that were on the ship.
_____

3. People were trying to get into the _____.

4. Which sister was older? _____

5. How old was that girl? _____

6. How old was her sister? _____

7. Linda told Kathy, "Hold on to my _____."

8. When the big man picked up Linda, where did he put her? _____

9. What country were the girls going to? _____

10. Why were the girls going there? _____

11. How long had they been on the ship? _____

Placement Guidelines

Use the table below to determine placement for each student.

Errors	Placement
If student makes seven errors or more on Part 1 **OR** three errors or more on Part 2	Place the student in a reading program more elementary than *Reading Mastery* Level 4
If a student makes no more than six errors on Part 1 **AND** no more than two errors on Part 2	Place the student at *Reading Mastery* Level 4, Lesson 1

If you suspect that some students are too advanced for the program (students who score 0 or 1 on the placement test and who exhibit good comprehension skills), present the main story from Lesson 103 to them. Present the tasks specified for the main story oral reading, and assign items 1–10 (17 responses) from Lesson 103 in the workbook.

If the student makes no more than eight story-reading errors and no more than two workbook errors on Lesson 103, place the student in a higher-level program, *Reading Mastery* Level 5.

Reading Mastery Level 5

Level 5 Placement Test Directions

Instructions for Part 1

Use the following procedures to administer part 1.

1. Give the student a blank copy of the Level 5 placement test. Use the student's copy to mark errors that the student makes.
2. Point to the passage and say: You're going to read this passage aloud. I want you to read it as well as you can. Don't try to read it so fast that you make mistakes, but don't read it so slowly that it doesn't make any sense. You have two minutes to read the passage. Go.
3. Time the student and make one tally mark for each error.
4. After two minutes, stop the student. Count every word not read as an error.
5. Total the student's errors.

Instructions for Part 2

After all the students have finished part 1, administer part 2 to the entire group. Use the following procedure.

1. Assemble the students.
2. Give each student a copy of the test, and make sure the students have pencils.
3. Say: Here is the passage that you read earlier. Read the passage again silently; then answer the questions in part 2. You have seven minutes. Go.
4. Collect the test papers after seven minutes.
5. Total each student's errors, using the answer key.

Answer Key for Part 2

1. Idea: *The Bermuda Islands.*
2. Ideas: *To dive; to see the bottom of the ocean.*
3. Response: *Warm.*
4. Response: *The guide.*
5. Ideas: *Partner; person.*
6. Idea: *Signal the guide.*
7. Idea: *Go to the surface of the water.*
8. Idea: *The diver might get the bends.*
9. Response: *Pressure.*

Placement Guidelines

Place your students as follows:

- Students who made zero errors or one error should be given the placement test for *Reading Mastery* Level 6.
- Students who made zero to six errors on part 1 *and* zero to two errors on part 2 can be placed in *Reading Mastery* Level 5.
- Students who made more than six errors on part 1 *or* more than two errors on part 2 should be given the placement test for *Reading Mastery* Level 4.

PLACEMENT TEST

Name _____

PART 1

An Underwater World

The diving boat was anchored in a place where the water changed from light green to dark, dark blue. One by one, the divers went down the ladder on the side of the boat and entered the warm water. The boat was about 1,600 kilometers east of Florida. They were south of the Bermuda Islands. Darla was the last diver to go down the ladder and enter the warm water.

"Now stick together," the guide said as he floated with his mask tilted back on his forehead. "You've got your partners. Stay with your partner. If you see something you want to look at, signal me. If one person stops, we all stop or somebody's going to get lost."

The guide continued, "If you get separated, go to the surface of the water. Don't try to look for the rest of us. Just go to the surface. And remember, don't go up too fast. Take at least two minutes to go up, or you may get the bends."

The bends. Darla had read about the bends. She knew that a person gets them because of the great pressure of the water.

PART 2

1. Near which islands does this story take place?

   _____

2. Why was the group in this place?

   _____

3. Was the water warm or cold?

   _____

4. Who led the group?

   _____

5. Each diver was supposed to stay with a

   _____.

6. What was a diver supposed to do if the diver wanted to stop to examine something?

   _____

7. What was a diver supposed to do if the diver got separated from the group?

   _____

8. What problem would the diver have if the diver went up to the surface too fast?

   _____

9. This problem was caused by the great

   _____ of the water.

Reading Mastery Level 6

Level 6 Placement Test Directions

Instructions for Part 1

Use the following procedures to administer Part 1.

1. Give the student a blank copy of the Level 6 placement test. Use the student's copy to mark errors that the student makes.
2. Point to the passage and say: You're going to read this passage aloud. I want you to read it as well as you can. Don't try to read it so fast that you make mistakes, but don't read it so slowly that it doesn't make any sense. You have two minutes to read the passage. Go.
3. Time the student and make one tally mark for each error.
4. After two minutes, stop the student. Count every word not read as an error.
5. Total the student's errors.

Instructions for Part 2

After all the students have finished part 1, administer part 2 to the entire group. Use the following procedure.

1. Assemble the students.
2. Give each student a copy of the placement test.
3. Say: Here is the passage that you read earlier. Read the passage again silently; then answer the questions in part 2. You have seven minutes. Go.
4. Collect the test papers after seven minutes.
5. Total each student's errors, using the answer key that follows.

Answer Key for Part 2

1. Response: *A king.*
2. Response: *A princess.*
3. Ideas: *His daughter; Marygold.*
4. Response: *Gold.*
5. Ideas: *His daughter; gold.*
6. Idea: *They weren't gold.*
7. Response: *Roses.*
8. Response: *Perfume.*
9. Idea: *How much it would be worth if the roses were gold.*

Placement Guidelines

Place your students as follows:

- Students who made zero to six errors on part 1 *and* zero to two errors on part 2 can be placed in *Reading Mastery* Level 6.
- Students who made more than six errors on part 1 *or* more than two errors on part 2 should be given the placement test for *Reading Mastery* Level 5.

PLACEMENT TEST

PART 1

The Golden Touch

Once upon a time in ancient Turkey there lived a rich king named Midas, who had a daughter named Marygold.

King Midas was very fond of gold. The only thing he loved more was his daughter. But the more Midas loved his daughter, the more he desired gold. He thought the best thing he could possibly do for his child would be to give her the largest pile of yellow, glistening coins that had ever been heaped together since the world began. So Midas gave all his thoughts and all his time to collecting gold.

When Midas gazed at the gold-tinted clouds of sunset, he wished they were real gold and that they could be herded into his strong box. When little Marygold ran to meet him with a bunch of buttercups and dandelions, he used to say, "Pooh, pooh, child. If these flowers were as golden as they look, they would be worth picking."

And yet, in his earlier days, before he had this insane desire for gold, Midas had shown a great love for flowers. He had planted a garden with the biggest and sweetest roses any person ever saw or smelled. These roses were still growing in the garden, as large, as lovely, and as fragrant as they were when Midas used to pass whole hours looking at them and inhaling their perfume. But now, if he looked at the flowers at all, it was only to calculate how much the garden would be worth if each of the rose petals was a thin plate of gold.

Name _____

PART 2

1. *Circle the answer.* What kind of royal person was Midas?
   • an emperor   • a king   • a prince

2. *Circle the answer.* So his daughter was ___.
   • an empress   • a queen   • a princess

3. What did Midas love most of all?
   _____

4. What did he love almost as much?
   _____

5. The more Midas loved _____,
   the more he desired _____.

6. Why did Midas think that dandelions were not worth picking?
   _____

7. What kind of flowers had Midas planted in his earlier days?
   _____

8. Midas used to inhale the _____
   of those flowers.

9. What did Midas think about his garden now?
   _____

Placement Test, Level 6   **81**

Sample Lessons

The following pages contain six sample lessons from *Reading Mastery* reproduced here in their entirety so that you can practice the skills discussed in this guide before presenting *Reading Mastery* to your students.

The first is Lesson 108 from *Reading Mastery I*. The second sample lesson is Lesson 76 from *Reading Mastery II*. Both lessons begin with word reading activities in the *Presentation Book*, followed by the *Storybook* reading, and ending with various activities in the *Take-Home Book*. These two lessons can be correlated *to Fast Cycle* lessons: *Reading Mastery I*, Lesson 108 corresponds to *Fast Cycle I*, Lesson 54; and *Reading Mastery II*, Lesson 76 corresponds to *Fast Cycle II*, Lesson 107.

Sample Lesson 3 is Lesson 71 from *Reading Mastery* Level 3. The fourth sample lesson is Lesson 21 from *Reading Mastery* Level 4. The fifth sample lesson is Lesson 76 from *Reading Mastery* Level 5. Students begin these lessons by reading word lists and a comprehension passage, followed by story reading in the *Textbook*. The students then work independently on the remaining *Workbook* and *Textbook* activities.

The sixth sample lesson is Lesson 57 from *Reading Mastery* Level 6. Students begin this lesson by reading word lists and vocabulary definitions. They then complete a skill exercise on making inferences. Afterward, the students read the first part of the classic story "A White Heron." Following the reading, they work independently on *Workbook* and *Textbook* activities.

Lesson 108

SOUNDS

p

TASK 1   Teaching p as in pat

a. Point to **p.** Here's a new sound. It's a quick sound.
b. My turn. (Pause.) Touch **p** for an instant, saying: p. *Do not say* **puuh.**
c. Again. Touch **p** and say: p.
d. Point to **p.** Your turn. When I touch it, you say it. (Pause.) Get ready. Touch **p.** *p.*
e. Again. Touch **p.** *p.*
f. Repeat *e* until firm.

TASK 2   Individual test

Call on different children to identify **p.**

t

g

TASK 3   Sounds firm-up

a. Get ready to say the sounds when I touch them.
b. Alternate touching **p** and **d.** Point to the sound. (Pause one second.) Say: Get ready. Touch the sound. *The children respond.*
c. When **p** and **d** are firm, alternate touching **p, g, d,** and **t** until all four sounds are firm.

TASK 4   Individual test

Call on different children to identify **p, g, d,** or **t.**

TASK 5   Sounds firm-up

a. Point to **p.** When I touch the sound, you say it.
b. (Pause.) Get ready. Touch **p.** *p.*
c. Again. Repeat *b* until firm.
d. Get ready to say all the sounds when I touch them.
e. Alternate touching **k, v, u, ō, p, sh, h,** and **n** three or four times. Point to the sound. (Pause one second.) Say: Get ready. Touch the sound. *The children respond.*

TASK 6   Individual test

Call on different children to identify one or more sounds in task 5.

108

READING VOCABULARY

TASK 7 Children rhyme with mop

a. Touch the ball for **mop.** You're going to read this word the
fast way. (Pause three seconds.) Get ready.
Move your finger quickly along the arrow. *Mop.*

b. Touch the ball for **cop.** This word rhymes with (pause) **mop.**
Move to **c,** then quickly along the arrow. *Cop.*
Yes, what word? (Signal.) *Cop.*

c. Touch the ball for **top.** This word rhymes with (pause) **mop.**
Move to **t,** then quickly along the arrow. *Top.*
Yes, what word? (Signal.) *Top.*

mop

cop

top

TASK 8 Children identify, then sound out an irregular word (was)

a. Touch the ball for **was.** Everybody, you're going to read this
word the fast way. (Pause three seconds.) Get ready.
Move your finger quickly along the arrow. *Was.* Yes, **was.**

b. Now you're going to sound out the word. Get ready.
Quickly touch **w, a, s** as the children say wwwaaasss.

c. Again. Repeat **b.**

d. How do we say the word? (Signal.) *Was.* Yes, **was.**

e. Repeat **b** and **d** until firm.

was

TASK 9 Individual test

Call on different children to do **b** and **d** in task 8.

TASK 10 Children read the fast way

Touch the ball for **ōld.** Get ready to read this word the fast way.
(Pause three seconds.) Get ready. (Signal.) *Old.*

ōld

TASK 11 Children read the words the fast way

Have the children read the words on this page the fast way.

TASK 12 Individual test

Call on different children to read one word the fast way.

2

108

Do not touch any small letters.

of

to

that

cōₐt

gōₐt

TASK 13   Children identify, then sound out an irregular word (of)

a. Touch the ball for **of**. Everybody, you're going to read this word the fast way. (Pause three seconds.) Get ready. Move your finger quickly along the arrow. *Of.* Yes, **of**.

b. Now you're going to sound out the word. Get ready. Quickly touch **o**, **f** as the children say *ooofff.*

c. Again. Repeat *b*.

d. How do we say the word? (Signal.) *Of.* Yes, **of**.

e. Repeat *b* and *d* until firm.

f. Call on different children to do *b* and *d*.

TASK 14   Children identify, then sound out an irregular word (to)

Repeat the procedures in task 13 for **to**.

TASK 15   Children read the fast way

Touch the ball for **that**. Get ready to read this word the fast way. (Pause three seconds.) Get ready. (Signal.) *That.*

TASK 16   Children sound out the word and tell what word

a. Touch the ball for **cōat**. Sound it out.

b. Get ready. Touch **c**, **ō**, **t** as the children say *cōōōt.*
    If sounding out is not firm, repeat *b*.

c. What word? (Signal.) *Coat.* Yes, **coat**.

TASK 17   Children sound out the word and tell what word

a. Touch the ball for **gōat**. Sound it out.

b. Get ready. Touch **g**, **ō**, **t** as the children say *gōōōt.*
    If sounding out is not firm, repeat *b*.

c. What word? (Signal.) *Goat.* Yes, **goat**.

TASK 18   Children read the words the fast way

Have the children read the words on this page the fast way.

TASK 19   Individual test

Call on different children to read one word the fast way.

3

Story 108

TASK 20   First reading—children read the story the fast way

Have the children reread any sentences containing words that give them trouble. Keep a list of these words.

a. Pass out Storybook 1.

b. Open your book to page 37 and get ready to read.

c. We're going to read this story the fast way.

d. Touch the first word. Check children's responses.

e. Reading the fast way. First word. (Pause three seconds.) Get ready. Clap. *Thē.*

f. Next word. Check children's responses. (Pause three seconds.) Get ready. Clap. *Old.*

g. Repeat *f* for the remaining words in the first sentence. Pause at least three seconds between claps. The children are to identify each word without sounding it out.

h. Repeat *d* through *g* for the next two sentences. Have the children reread the first three sentences until firm.

i. The children are to read the remainder of the story the fast way, stopping at the end of each sentence.

j. After the first reading of the story, print on the board the words that the children missed more than one time. Have the children sound out each word one time and tell what word.

k. After the group's responses are firm, call on individual children to read the words.

TASK 21   Individual test

a. I'm going to call on different children to read a whole sentence the fast way. Do not clap for each word.

b. Call on different children to read a sentence. Do not clap for each word.

TASK 22   Second reading—children read the story the fast way and answer questions

a. You're going to read the story again the fast way and I'll ask questions.

b. First word. Check children's responses. Get ready. Clap. *Thē.*

c. Clap for each remaining word. Pause at least three seconds between claps. Pause longer before words that gave the children trouble during the first reading.

d. Ask the comprehension questions below as the children read.

After the children read:	You ask:
The old goat had an old coat.	**What did she have?** (Signal.) *An old coat.*
The old goat said, "I will eat this old coat."	**What did she say?** (Signal.) *I will eat this old coat.*
So she did.	**What did she do?** (Signal.) *She ate the old coat.*
"That was fun," she said.	**What did she say?** (Signal.) *That was fun.*
"I ate the old coat."	**What did the goat say?** (Signal.) *I ate the old coat.*
"And now I am cold."	**What did she say?** (Signal.) *And now I am cold.*
Now the old goat is sad.	**How does she feel?** (Signal.) *Sad.* **Why?** (Signal.) *The children respond.*

TASK 23   Picture comprehension

a. What do you think you'll see in the picture? *The children respond.*

b. Turn the page and look at the picture.

c. Ask these questions:

1. How does that goat feel? *The children respond.   Cold and sad.*

2. Why is she out in the cold without a coat? *The children respond.   Because she ate her coat.*

3. Did you ever go outside without a coat when it was cold? *The children respond.*

4

Take-Home 108

SUMMARY OF INDEPENDENT ACTIVITY

TASK 24 Introduction to independent activity

a. Pass out Take-Home 108 to each child.

b. Everybody, you're going to do this take-home on your own.
Tell the children when they will work the items.
Let's go over the things you're going to do.

TASK 25 Sentence copying

a. Hold up side 1 of your take-home and point to the first line in the sentence-copying exercise.

b. Everybody, here's the sentence you're going to write on the lines below.

c. Get ready to read the words in this sentence the fast way.
First word. Check children's responses. Get ready. Clap. *Thē.*
Next word. Check children's responses. Get ready. Clap. *Goat.*

d. Next word. Check children's responses. Get ready.

e. Repeat *d* for the remaining words.

f. After you finish your take-home, you get to draw a picture about the sentence, **thē gōat āte thē cōat.**

TASK 26 Sound writing

a. Point to the sound-writing exercise. Here are the sounds you're going to write today. I'll touch the sounds. You say them.

b. Touch each sound. *The children respond.*

c. Repeat the series until firm.

TASK 27 Matching

a. Point to the column of words in the Matching Game.

b. Everybody, you're going to follow the lines and write these words.

c. Reading the fast way.

d. Point to the first word. (Pause.) Get ready. (Signal.) *The children respond.*

e. Repeat *d* for the remaining words.

f. Repeat *d* and *e* until firm.

TASK 28 Cross-out game

Point to the boxed word in the Cross-out Game. Everybody, here's the word you're going to cross out today. What word? (Signal.) *Not.* Yes, **not.**

TASK 29 Pair relations

a. Point to the pair-relations exercise on side 2. You're going to circle the picture in each box that shows what the words say.

b. Point to the space at the top of the page. After you finish, remember to draw a picture that shows **thē gōat āte thē cōat.**

INDIVIDUAL CHECKOUT: STORYBOOK

TASK 30 2½-minute individual checkout — whole story

Make a permanent chart for recording results of individual checkouts. See Teacher's Guide for sample chart.

a. As you are doing your take-home, I'll call on children one at a time to read the **whole story.** If you can read the whole story the fast way in less than two and a half minutes and if you make no more than three errors, I'll put two stars after your name on the chart for lesson 108.

b. If you make too many errors or don't read the story in less than two and a half minutes, you'll have to practice it and do it again. When you do read it in under two and a half minutes with no more than three errors, you'll get one star. Remember, two stars if you can do it the first time, one star if you do it the second or third time you try.

c. Call on a child. Tell the child: Read the whole story very carefully the fast way. Go. Time the child. If the child makes a mistake, quickly tell the child the correct word and permit the child to continue reading. As soon as the child makes more than three errors or exceeds the time limit, tell the child to stop. You'll have to read the story to yourself and try again later. Plan to monitor the child's practice.

d. Record two stars for each child who reads appropriately. Congratulate those children.

e. Give children who do not earn two stars a chance to read the story again before the next lesson is presented. Award one star to each of those children who meet the rate and accuracy criterion.

41 words/2.5 min = 16 wpm [3 errors]

END OF LESSON 108

5

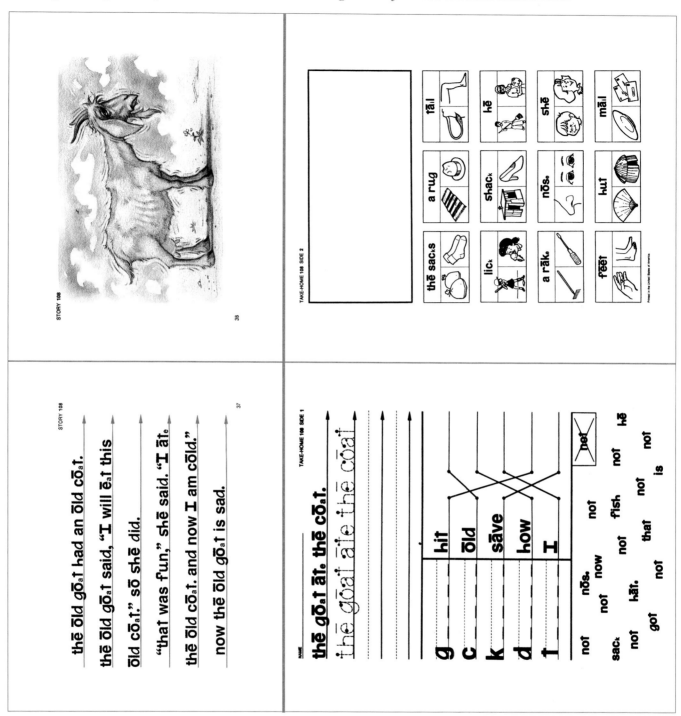

STORY 108

38

the ōld gōₐt had an ōld cōₐt.

the ōld gōₐt said, "I will ēₐt this ōld cōₐt." sō shē did.

"that was fun," shē said. "I āte the ōld cōₐt. and now I am cōld."

now the ōld gōₐt is sad.

STORY 108

37

NAME

TAKE-HOME 108 SIDE 1

the gōₐt āte the cōₐt.

the gōat ate the coat

g   hit
c   ōld
k   sāve
d   how
t   I

not   nōsₑ
sacₖ   not   now   not   fish   not   hē
        got   hātₑ   that   not   not
                                is

TAKE-HOME 108 SIDE 2

the sacₖs   a rug   tāil

licₖ   shacₖ   hē

a rākₑ   nōsₑ   shē

fēēt   hut   māil

LESSON 76

READING VOCABULARY
Do not touch small letters.
Get ready to read all the words on this page
without making a mistake.

TASK 1 Sound out first

best

a. Touch the ball for **best**. Sound it out. Get ready. Quickly touch **b**, **e**, **s**, **t** as the children say *beeessst*.
b. What word? (Signal.) *Best.* Yes, **best**.
c. Repeat task until firm.

ing

TASK 2 ing words

something

a. Point to **ing**. When these letters are together, they usually say **ing**.
b. What do these letters usually say? (Signal.) *ing.* Yes, **ing**. Repeat until firm.
c. Point to the words. These are words you already know. See if you can read them when they look this way.

looking

d. Point to **ing** in **something**. What do these letters say? (Signal.) *ing.*
e. Touch the ball for **something**. Read the fast way. Get ready. (Signal.) *Something.* Yes, **something**.

rēading

f. Repeat *d* and *e* for **looking** and **rēading**.
g. Repeat the series of words until firm.

parts

TASK 3 ar word

a. Touch the ball for **parts**. Read this word the fast way. (Pause two seconds.) Get ready. (Signal.) *Parts.* Yes, **parts**.
b. Point to **ar** in **parts**. Everybody, what do these letters say? (Signal.) *Are.* Yes, **are**.
c. Touch the ball for **parts**. Sound it out. Get ready. Quickly touch **p**, **ar**, **t**, **s** as the children say *partsss*.
d. What word? (Signal.) *Parts.* Yes, **parts**.
e. Repeat *c* and *d* until firm.

kites

TASK 4 Practice final-e rule

a. Read this word the fast way. Remember to look at the end of the word.
b. Touch the ball for **kites**. (Pause two seconds.) Get ready. (Signal.) *Kites.* Yes, **kites**.
c. Touch the ball for **kites**. Sound it out. Get ready. Quickly touch **k**, **i**, **t**, **s** as the children say *kiiitsss*.
d. What word? (Signal.) *Kites.* Yes, **kites**.
e. Repeat *b* through *d* until firm.

Repeat any troublesome words.

Individual test
Call on different children. Each child reads a different word.

76

Do not touch small letters.
Get ready to read all the words on this page
without making a mistake.

TASK 5   Read the fast way

a. Read these words the fast way.

b. Touch the ball for **store**. (Pause two
seconds.) Get ready. (Signal.) *Store.* Yes,
store.

c. Repeat *b* for **make, makes, making, home,
pāper, what, when, then, who, how, from,
began, other, else,** and **next.**

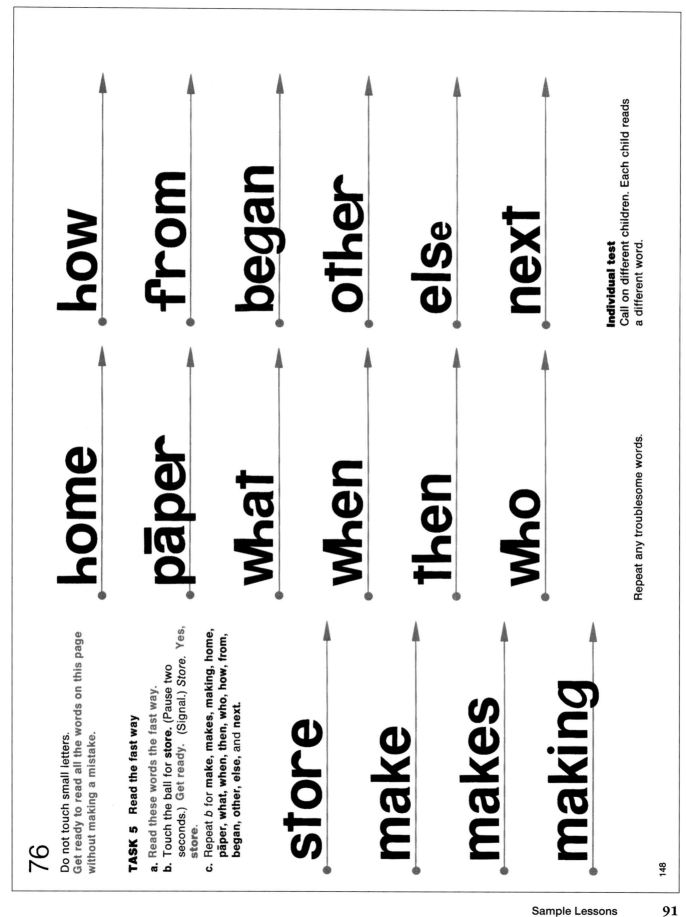

Individual test
Call on different children. Each child reads
a different word.

Repeat any troublesome words.

148

76

Get ready to read all the words on this page without making a mistake.

TASK 6 Long and short vowel words

a. Read these words the fast way. Remember to look at the end of the word.

b. Touch the ball for **rode.** (Pause two seconds.) Get ready. (Signal.) *Rode.* Yes, rode.

c. Repeat *b* for **kite, sam, not, same, rod, note,** and **kit.**

not

same

rod

note

kit

rode

kite

sam

Individual test

Call on individual children to read a column of words from this lesson. If the column contains only one or two words, direct the child to read additional words from an adjacent column.

STORYBOOK

STORY 76

TASK 7 First reading—title and three sentences

a. Pass out Storybook 1.

b. Everybody, open your reader to page 200.

c. Everybody, touch the title of the story and get ready to read the words in the title.

d. First word. Check children's responses. Get ready. Clap. *Sam.*

e. Clap for each remaining word in the title.

f. Everybody, say the title. (Signal.) *Sam gets a kite kit.*

g. Everybody, get ready to read this story.

h. First word. Check children's responses. Get ready. Clap. *Sam.*

i. Next word. Check children's responses. Get ready. Clap. *Liked.*

j. Repeat *i* for the remaining words in the first three sentences. Have the children reread the first three sentences until firm.

149

76

TASK 8 Remaining sentences

a. I'm going to call on different children to read a sentence. Everybody, follow along and point to the words. If you hear a mistake, raise your hand.

b. Call on a child. Read the next sentence.

To correct word-identification errors (**from,** for example)

1. That word is **from.** What word? *From.*

2. Go back to the beginning of the sentence and read the sentence again.

c. Call on a different child. Read the next sentence.

d. Repeat *c* for most of the remaining sentences in the story.

e. Occasionally have the group read a sentence.

When the group is to read, say: Everybody, read the next sentence. Clap for each word in the sentence.

> ## sam gets a kite kit[1]
>
> sam liked to make things. he liked to make toy cars. so he went to the store and got a toy car kit.[2] his mom said, "that kit has the parts of a car. you have to rēad and fīnd out how to fit the parts so that they make a car."
>
> sam said, "I will do that."
>
> so sam began to rēad the pāper that came with the car kit.[3] then he began to fit the parts to make a car. soon he had a toy car.
>
> his mom said, "that is a fine car. you are good at rēading and at making things."[4]
>
> sam did not like to make the same thing again. he said, "I will not make other cars. I will make something else."
>
> so he went to the store and got a kite kit.[5] when he got home, he shōwed his mom the kite kit. his mom said, "that kit has a lot of parts in it. you will have to rēad the pāper that comes with the kit to fīnd out how to make the kite."[6]

TASK 9 Second reading—sentences and questions

a. You're going to read the story again. This time I'm going to ask questions.

b. Starting with the first word of the title. Check children's responses. Get ready. Clap as the children read the title.

c. Call on a child. Read the first sentence.

To correct word-identification errors (**from,** for example)

1. That word is **from.** What word? *From.*

2. Go back to the beginning of the sentence and read the sentence again.

d. Call on a different child. Read the next sentence.

e. Repeat *d* for most of the remaining sentences in the story.

f. Occasionally have the group read a sentence.

g. After each underlined sentence has been read, present each comprehension question specified below to the entire group.

[1] What will Sam get? (Signal.) *A kite kit.* What is a kite kit? *The children respond.* Yes, in a kite kit you get all the parts to build a kite.

[2] What kind of kit did he get? (Signal.) *A toy car kit.* What is he going to make? (Signal.) *A toy car.*

[3] Why does he have to read the paper? *The children respond.* Right, the paper tells him how to make the car.

[4] Everybody, say that. (Signal.) *You are good at reading and at making things.*

[5] What did he get this time? (Signal.) *A kite kit.*

[6] Why does he have to read the paper? *The children respond.* Right, the paper tells him how to make the kite.

150

76

sam looked inside the kit. then he said, "what pāper? there is no pāper in this kit."

sam's mom said, "that is too bad. how will you make the kite if there is no pāper in the kit?"

sam said, "I will go back to the store and get a pāper that tells how to make a kite from these parts."

when sam got to the store, the man in the store said, "I dōn't have other pāpers that tell how to make kites."

sam asked, "how can I make a kite if I dōn't have the pāper?"[8]

the man said, "you will have to do the best you can."[9]

sam was not happy. he went home and looked at all the parts in the kite kit.

more to come[10]

[7]Was there a paper in the kit? (Signal.) No. I wonder how he'll make the kite without that paper. *The children respond.* Let's read and find out.
[8]Everybody, say that question. (Signal.) *How can I make a kite if I don't have the paper?*
[9]Everybody, say the man's answer. (Signal.) *You will have to do the best you can.*
[10]We'll read more next time.

TASK 10   Picture comprehension

a. Look at the picture.
b. Ask these questions:
1. Point to the toy car. Who made that car? (Signal.) *Sam.*
2. Why did Sam make that car? (Signal.) *He likes to make things.*
3. Point to the kite parts. What is that stuff on the floor? *The children respond.* Yes, those are the kite parts.
4. Can you see a paper telling Sam how to make the kite? (Signal.) *No.* Why not? *The children respond.* Right, the paper is missing. I hope he can put all those parts together.

TAKE-HOME 76

SUMMARY OF INDEPENDENT ACTIVITY

TASK 11   Introduction to independent activity

a. Pass out Take-Home 76 to each child.
b. Hold up side 1 of your take-home. Everybody, you're going to do this take-home on your own. Tell the children when they will work the items. Let's go over the things you're going to do.

TASK 12   Story items

Point to the story-items exercise. Everybody, remember to write your answers in the blanks.

TASK 13   Following instructions

a. Touch the sentence in the box.
b. Everybody, first you're going to read the sentence in the box. Then you're going to read the instructions below the box and do what the instructions tell you to do.

TASK 14   Story-picture items

Point to the story-picture items on side 2. Remember to follow these instructions and look at the picture when you work these items.

TASK 15   Reading comprehension

Point to the story. You're going to read this story and then do the items. Remember to write the answers in the blanks.

END OF LESSON 76

sam gets a kite kit

sam liked to make things. he liked to make toy cars. so he went to the store and got a toy car kit. his mom said, "that kit has the parts of a car. you have to read and find out how to fit the parts so that they make a car."

sam said, "I will do that."

so sam began to read the paper that came with the car kit. then he began to fit the parts to make a car. soon he had a toy car.

his mom said, "that is a fine car. you are good at reading and at making things."

sam did not like to make the same thing again. he said, "I will

not make other cars. I will make something else."

so he went to the store and got a kite kit. when he got home, he showed his mom the kite kit. his mom said, "that kit has a lot of parts in it. you will have to read the paper that comes with the kit to find out how to make the kite."

sam looked inside the kit. then he said, "what paper? there is no paper in this kit."

sam's mom said, "that is too bad. how will you make the kite if there is no paper in the kit?"

sam said, "I will go back to the store and get a paper that tells how to make a kite from these parts."

STORY **76**

203

when sam got to the store, the man in the store said, "I dōn't have other pāpers that tell how to make kites."

sam asked, "how can I make a kite if I dōn't have the pāper?"

the man said, "you will have to do the best you can."

sam was not happy. he went home and looked at all the parts in the kite kit.

more to come

STORY **76**

202

TAKE-HOME **76**   SIDE **2**

look at the picture on page 203 of your reader.

1. is sam reading a paper? ___

2. do you see sam's toy car? ___

bob got a kit for making a toy duck. the kit had a lot of parts. bob worked hard. at last, he said, "that duck looks real." the duck ate a hole in the wall. then he ate some grass. the duck went to the pond and swam away.

1. who got a kit for making a toy duck? ___

2. the duck ate a hole in the ___.

3. then he ate some ___.

4. where did he go for a swim? ___

NAME ___

TAKE-HOME **76**   SIDE **1**

1. who made a toy car from a car kit? ___

2. who said, "you are good at reading and at making things"? his ___

3. what kit did sam get after he made a car? a ___
   • car kit   • cat kit   • kite kit   • log kit

4. what was missing from the kit? a ___
   • paper   • kite part   • car part   • kit

5. where did sam go to get a paper? ___
   • to the lake   • to the store
   • because he needed it   • told him

6. did the man at the store have another paper? ___

tim went to the park.

1. circle the word that tells who went to the park.

2. make a line over the words that tell where tim went.

3. make a line over the circle.

Lesson 71

EXERCISE 1
VOCABULARY REVIEW

a. You learned a sentence that tells how long she survived.
- Everybody, say that sentence. Get ready. (Signal.) *She survived until she was rescued.*
- (Repeat until firm.)

b. You learned a sentence that tells what the soldiers did.
- Say that sentence. Get ready. (Signal.) *The soldiers protected their equipment.*
- (Repeat until firm.)

c. Here's the last sentence you learned: Lawyers with talent normally succeed.
- Everybody, say that sentence. Get ready. (Signal.) *Lawyers with talent normally succeed.*
- (Repeat until firm.)

d. Everybody, what do we call people who help us when we have questions about the law? (Signal.) *Lawyers.*
- What's another word for **usually?** (Signal.) *Normally.*
- What word refers to the special skills a person has? (Signal.) *Talent.*
- What word means the opposite of **fail?** (Signal.) *Succeed.*

e. Once more. Say the sentence that tells about lawyers with talent. Get ready. (Signal.) *Lawyers with talent normally succeed.*

EXERCISE 2
READING WORDS

Column 1

a. **Find lesson 71 in your textbook.** ✓
- Touch column 1. ✓
- (Teacher reference:)

1. **Mr. Daniels**	4. **medicine**
2. **recognize**	5. **guess**
3. **elevator**	6. **dozen**

b. Number 1 is the name **Mr. Daniels.** What name? (Signal.) *Mr. Daniels.*

c. Word 2 is **recognize.** What word? (Signal.) *Recognize.*

- When you **recognize** something that you see or feel, you know what it is. Here's another way of saying **She knew what the smell was: She recognized the smell.**

d. Your turn. What's another way of saying **She knew what the smell was?** (Signal.) *She recognized the smell.*
- (Repeat step d until firm.)

e. What's another way of saying **She knew who the person was?** (Signal.) *She recognized the person.*

f. Word 3 is **elevator.** What word? (Signal.) *Elevator.*
- Spell **elevator.** Get ready. (Tap for each letter.) *E-L-E-V-A-T-O-R.*

g. Word 4 is **medicine.** What word? (Signal.) *Medicine.*
- Spell **medicine.** Get ready. (Tap for each letter.) *M-E-D-I-C-I-N-E.*

h. Word 5 is **guess.** What word? (Signal.) *Guess.*
- Spell **guess.** Get ready. (Tap for each letter.) *G-U-E-S-S.*

i. Word 6 is **dozen.** What word? (Signal.) *Dozen.*
- Spell **dozen.** Get ready. (Tap for each letter.) *D-O-Z-E-N.*

j. Let's read those words again, the fast way.
- Number 1. What words? (Signal.) *Mr. Daniels.*

k. Word 2. What word? (Signal.) *Recognize.*
- (Repeat for words 3–6.)

l. (Repeat steps j and k until firm.)

Column 2

m. Find column 2. ✓
- (Teacher reference:)

1. **silently**	4. **approached**
2. **watering**	5. **fairly**
3. **heater**	

- All these words have endings.

n. Word 1. What word? (Signal.) *Silently.*
- (Repeat for words 2–5.)

o. (Repeat step n until firm.)

Column 3

p. Find column 3. ✓
• (Teacher reference:)

1. clues	4. drugs
2. doctors	5. typists
3. offices	6. lawyers

• All these words end with the letter **S.**
q. Word 1. What word? (Signal.) *Clues.*
  ⌐• (Repeat for words 2–6.)
  └ r. (Repeat step q until firm.)

Column 4

s. Find column 4. ✓
• (Teacher reference:)

1. cock your head	4. refinery
2. equipment	5. friendly
3. motorcycle	6. unfriendly

t. Number 1. What words? (Signal.) *Cock your head.*
• When you cock your head, you tilt it. Everybody, show me how you cock your head. ✓
⌐u. Word 2. What word? (Signal.) *Equipment.*
└• (Repeat for words 3–6.)
⌐v. Let's read those words again.
│• Number 1. What words? (Signal.) *Cock your head.*
⌐w. Word 2. What word? (Signal.) *Equipment.*
│└• (Repeat for words 3–6.)
└x. (Repeat steps v and w until firm.)

Column 5

y. Find column 5. ✓
• (Teacher reference:)

1. explain	4. crude
2. insist	5. fifth
3. honest	

z. Word 1. What word? (Signal.) *Explain.*
• When you **explain** something, you **tell about it.** Here's another way of saying **She told about her talent: She explained her talent.**
⌐a. Your turn. What's another way of saying **She told about her talent?** (Signal.) *She explained her talent.*
└• (Repeat step a until firm.)

b. What's another way of saying **He told about his plan?** (Signal.) *He explained his plan.*
⌐c. Word 2. What word? (Signal.) *Insist.*
└• (Repeat for words 3–5.)
⌐d. Let's read those words again.
│• Word 1. What word? (Signal.) *Explain.*
│• (Repeat for words 2–5.)
└e. (Repeat step d until firm.)

Column 6

f. Find column 6. ✓
• (Teacher reference:)

1. narrow	4. several
2. prison	5. pipeline
3. polite	

⌐g. Word 1. What word? (Signal.) *Narrow.*
│• (Repeat for words 2–5.)
└h. (Repeat step g until firm.)

Individual Turns

(For columns 1–6: Call on individual students, each to read one to three words per turn.)

EXERCISE 3

COMPREHENSION PASSAGE

a. Find part B in your textbook. ✓
• You're going to read the next story about Bertha. First you'll read the information passage. It gives some facts about wells.
b. Everybody, touch the title. ✓
• (Call on a student to read the title.) *[Oil Wells.]*
• Everybody, what's the title? (Signal.) *Oil Wells.*
c. (Call on individual students to read the passage, each student reading two or three sentences at a time. Ask the specified questions as the students read.)

Oil Wells

  A well is a deep hole in the ground. The well has pipe in it so the hole stays open.

• Why does the well have a pipe in it? (Call on a student. Idea: *So the hole stays open.*)

There are different types of wells.
• Some wells are fresh-water wells. These wells pump fresh water from under the ground.

• What do fresh-water wells do? (Call on a student. Idea: *Pump fresh water from under the ground.*)

• Some wells are oil wells. These wells pump crude oil from under the ground.

• What do oil wells do? (Call on a student. Idea: *Pump crude oil from under the ground.*)

Picture 1 shows a machine that is drilling a hole for a well.

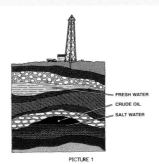

FRESH WATER
CRUDE OIL
SALT WATER

PICTURE 1

• Everybody, touch the underground pipe in picture 1 and show how far down the well is already dug. ✓

If the machine keeps drilling, what type of liquid will it reach first?

• Everybody, touch the liquid it will reach first. ✓
• What kind of liquid is that? (Signal.) *Fresh water.*

If the machine keeps drilling past the fresh water, what kind of liquid will it reach next?

• Everybody, touch the liquid it will reach next. ✓
• What kind of liquid is that? (Signal.) *Crude oil.*

If the machine keeps drilling, what will it reach after the oil?

• Everybody, touch the liquid it will reach next. ✓
• What kind of liquid is that? (Signal.) *Salt water.*
• If you dig a well deep enough, you'll always hit salt water.

If the well is an oil well, it pumps crude oil from the ground. Crude oil is a dark liquid that can be changed to make things like gasoline, motor oil, and plastic.

• What can be made from crude oil? (Call on a student.) *Gasoline, motor oil, plastic.*

The crude oil is pumped from the well. Then it goes into a pipeline.

• Everybody, where does the crude oil go from the well? (Signal.) *Into a pipeline.*

The pipeline goes along the ground and carries the crude oil many miles to a refinery.

• Everybody, where does the pipeline take the crude oil? (Signal.) *To a refinery.*
• Is the refinery usually right next to the well? (Signal.) *No.*

The refinery is a large place with strange-looking equipment and large tanks for holding oil.
The refinery changes crude oil into gasoline and other things.

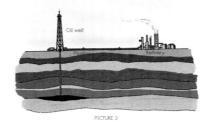

Oil well
Refinery

PICTURE 2

• What does the refinery do? (Call on a student. Idea: *Changes crude oil into gasoline and other things.*)
• Everybody, touch the crude oil underground in picture 2. ✓
• Now follow it up the pipe to the surface of the ground. ✓
• Now follow it in the pipeline to the other end of the pipeline. ✓

118 *Lesson 71*

- What's the other end? (Signal.) *The refinery.*
- What does that refinery do to the crude oil? (Call on a student. Idea: *Changes it into gasoline and other things.*)
- The oil company that you're reading about is a refinery.

<hr/>

EXERCISE 4

STORY READING

a. Find part C in your textbook. ✓
  - The error limit for this story is 9. Read carefully.
b. Everybody, touch the title. ✓
  - (Call on a student to read the title.) *[Maria Tests Bertha's Talent.]*
  - What's going to happen in this story? (Call on a student. Idea: *Maria will test Bertha's talent.*)
c. (Call on individual students to read the story, each student reading two or three sentences at a time. Ask questions marked 1.)

> - (Correct errors: Tell the word. Direct the student to reread the sentence.)
> - (If the group makes more than 9 errors, direct the students to reread the story.)

d. (After the group has read the selection making no more than 9 errors, read the story to the students and ask questions marked 2.)

Maria Tests Bertha's Talent

Bertha had a plan for helping Maria figure out where the water came from. You probably know what her plan was.

1. What do you think it was? (Call on a student. Idea: *Get water from the oil company and have Bertha smell it to see whether it came from the creek or water wells.*)

Although Bertha didn't know too much about oil wells and refineries, she did know that she could smell the difference between water taken from the creek and water taken from water wells.

2. Everybody, where was the company supposed to be taking water from? (Signal.) *Wells.*

2. Where did Maria think it was coming from? (Signal.) *The creek.*

Bertha was sitting on Maria's porch. She said, "Maria, it's easy for me to tell if the water comes from the creek or from the well. I'll just smell it."
Maria looked slowly at Bertha and made a face. "What are you talking about?"

1. Everybody, show me the kind of face Maria probably made. ✓
1. What was Maria thinking about Bertha? (Call on a student. Idea: *That she was strange or crazy.*)

Bertha said, "Take me with you and I'll tell you where the water comes from."
Maria made another face. "How will you know where it comes from?"
"I told you. I'll smell it," Bertha said. Then she explained her talent.

1. How would she do that? (Call on a student. Idea: *By telling Maria how she used her sense of smell.*)

"I can tell about anything by smelling it. Honest I can."
Maria cocked her head and looked at Bertha.

2. Everybody, show me how you cock your head. ✓

"What is this, a joke?" Maria asked.
Bertha said, "Give me a test. Get glasses of water from different places. I'll tell you where you got each glass of water." At first Maria didn't want to do it. "This is crazy," she kept saying. But Bertha kept insisting on the test.

2. What would she say to keep insisting on the test? (Call on a student. Idea: *Get glasses of water from different places and I'll tell you where each one came from.*)

Finally Maria went into her house and came back with three glasses of water. She said, "You can't feel them, or you may get some clues about where I got them."

2. What kind of clues could you get by feeling the water glasses? (Call on a student. Idea: *Clues about temperature.*)

Bertha said, "I don't have to feel them. The one on the left is from your water heater.

2. What's a water heater? (Call on a student. Idea: *A machine that makes cold water get hot.*)

The middle glass is from a watering can or something like that.

2. What do you do with a watering can? (Call on a student. Idea: *Water plants and flowers.*)

That water has been sitting out for a couple of days. The water in the last glass came from a water jug or something in your refrigerator. It's been in the refrigerator for a long time, and it probably doesn't taste very good."
"I don't believe this," Maria said, and she tasted the water from the last glass. She made a face. "Oh, you're right. It's bad."

2. Everybody, show me the kind of face she made when she tasted the water. ✓

Suddenly Maria laughed, turned around, and looked at Bertha. She said, "I don't believe this." Then she said, "I don't believe this," three or four more times. "You're amazing. You are amazing. You are the most amazing person I have ever seen."
She kept talking very fast. She told about some of the amazing things that she had seen—a cow with two heads and a building over 3 hundred meters high. Finally, she said, "I once saw a man jump a motorcycle over twenty cars and that was amazing, but you are five times as amazing."

2. Maria is really excited. I'll read that part again. Listen to how she talks on and on.

Suddenly Maria laughed, turned around, and looked at Bertha. She said, "I don't believe this." Then she said, "I don't believe this," three or four more times. "You're amazing. You are amazing. You are the most amazing person I have ever seen."
She kept talking very fast. She told about some of the amazing things that she had seen—a cow with two heads and a building over 3 hundred meters high. Finally, she said, "I once saw a man jump a motorcycle over twenty cars and that was amazing, but you are five times as amazing."

"Can I go with you?" Bertha asked. "Yes, yes, yes, yes, yes," Maria said. "This will be great."
MORE NEXT TIME

1. Go back to the beginning of the story. Follow along while I read.
2. What do you think is going to happen? (Call on a student. Idea: *Maria will get Bertha to smell the water the oil company uses;* etc.)

EXERCISE 5

PAIRED PRACTICE

You're going to read aloud to your partner. Today the **B** members will read first. Then the **A** members will read from the star to the end of the story.
(Observe students and give feedback.)

End-of-Lesson Activities

INDEPENDENT WORK

Now finish your independent work for lesson 71. Raise your hand when you're finished. (Observe students and give feedback.)

WORKCHECK

a. (Direct students to take out their marking pencils.)
• We're going to check your independent work. Remember, if you got an item wrong, make an **X** next to the item. Don't change any answers.

b. (For each item: Read the item. Call on a student to answer it. If the answer is wrong, say the correct answer. Refer to the Answer Key for the correct answers.)

c. Now use your marking pencil to fix up any items you got wrong. Remember, all mistakes must be fixed up before you hand in your independent work.

WRITING-SPELLING

(Present Writing-Spelling lesson 71 after completing Reading lesson 71. See Writing-Spelling Guide.)

LANGUAGE ARTS GUIDE

(Present Language Arts lesson 71 after completing Reading lesson 71. See Language Arts Guide.)

The *Language Arts Guide* is not a core component of *Reading Mastery* Classic.

Lesson 71 **121**

• Some wells are oil wells. These wells pump crude oil from under the ground.

Picture 1 shows a machine that is drilling a hole for a well.

If the machine keeps drilling, what type of liquid will it reach first?

If the machine keeps drilling past the fresh water, what kind of liquid will it reach next?

If the machine keeps drilling, what will it reach after the oil?

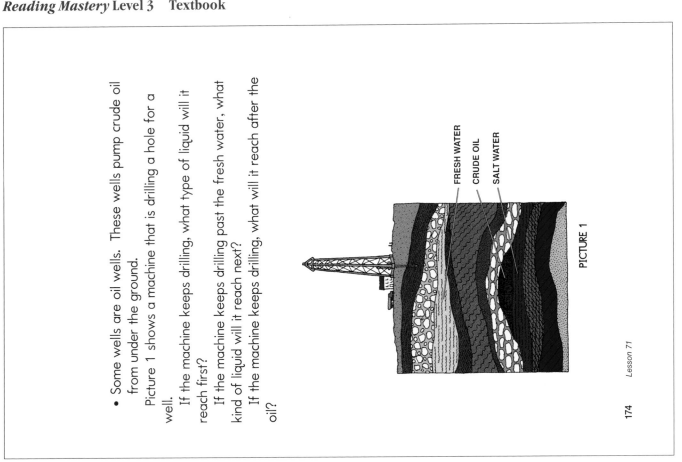

FRESH WATER
CRUDE OIL
SALT WATER

PICTURE 1

174   *Lesson 71*

71

1
1. Mr. Daniels
2. recognize
3. elevator
4. medicine
5. guess
6. dozen

2
1. silently
2. watering
3. heater
4. approached
5. fairly

3
1. clues
2. doctors
3. offices
4. drugs
5. typists
6. lawyers

4
1. cock your head
2. equipment
3. motorcycle
4. refinery
5. friendly
6. unfriendly

5
1. explain
2. insist
3. honest
4. crude
5. fifth

6
1. narrow
2. prison
3. polite
4. several
5. pipeline

B

Oil Wells

A well is a deep hole in the ground. The well has pipe in it so the hole stays open. There are different types of wells.

• Some wells are fresh-water wells. These wells pump fresh water from under the ground.

Lesson 71   173

If the well is an oil well, it pumps crude oil from the ground. Crude oil is a dark liquid that can be changed to make things like gasoline, motor oil, and plastic.

The crude oil is pumped from the well. Then it goes into a pipeline. The pipeline goes along the ground and carries the crude oil many miles to a refinery.

The refinery is a large place with strange-looking equipment and large tanks for holding oil.

The refinery changes crude oil into gasoline and other things.

Oil well

Refinery

Pipeline

PICTURE 2

Lesson 71   175

C Maria Tests Bertha's Talent

Bertha had a plan for helping Maria figure out where the water came from. You probably know what her plan was. Although Bertha didn't know too much about oil wells and refineries, she did know that she could smell the difference between water taken from the creek and water taken from water wells.

Bertha was sitting on Maria's porch. She said, "Maria, it's easy for me to tell if the water comes from the creek or from the well. I'll just smell it."

Maria looked slowly at Bertha and made a face. "What are you talking about?"

Bertha said, "Take me with you and I'll tell you where the water comes from."

Maria made another face. "How will you know where it comes from?"

"I told you. I'll smell it," Bertha said. Then she explained her talent. "I can tell about anything by smelling it. Honest I can."

Maria cocked her head and looked at Bertha. "What is this, a joke?" Maria asked.

Bertha said, "Give me a test. Get glasses of water from different places. I'll tell you where you got each glass of water." At first Maria didn't want to do it. "This is crazy," she kept saying. But Bertha kept insisting on the test. Finally Maria went into her house and came back with three

176   *Lesson 71*

D Number your paper from 1 through 19.

Skill Items

Lawyers with talent normally succeed.

1. What word means the opposite of **fail?**
2. What word names people who help us when we have questions about the law?
3. What word means **usually?**
4. What word refers to the special skills a person has?

Review Items

5. You can see drops of water on grass early in the morning. What are those called?

6. Which letter shows the coconut milk?
7. Which letter shows the inner shell?
8. Which letter shows the coconut meat?
9. Which letter shows the outer shell?

178   *Lesson 71*

---

glasses of water. She said, "You ⭐ can't feel them, or you may get some clues about where I got them."

Bertha said, "I don't have to feel them. The one on the left is from your water heater. The middle glass is from a watering can or something like that. That water has been sitting out for a couple of days. The water in the last glass came from a water jug or something in your refrigerator. It's been in the refrigerator for a long time, and it probably doesn't taste very good."

"I don't believe this," Maria said, and she tasted the water from the last glass. She made a face. "Oh, you're right. It's bad."

Suddenly Maria laughed, turned around, and looked at Bertha. She said, "I don't believe this." Then she said, "I don't believe this," three or four more times. "You're amazing. You are amazing. You are the most amazing person I have ever seen."

She kept talking very fast. She told about some of the amazing things that she had seen—a cow with two heads and a building over 3 hundred meters high. Finally, she said, "I once saw a man jump a motorcycle over twenty cars and that that was amazing, but you are five times as amazing."

"Can I go with you?" Bertha asked.

"Yes, yes, yes, yes," Maria said. "This will be great."

MORE NEXT TIME

Lesson 71   177

15. Write the letter that shows a tugboat.
16. Write two letters that show ships.
17. Write two letters that show docks.

18. The place that is called Troy is now part of what country?
    - Greece   - Italy   - Turkey
19. Write the letters of the **4** kinds of weapons that soldiers used when they had battles with Troy.

a. bows   c. arrows   e. spears   g. planes
b. swords   d. rockets   f. guns   h. tanks

180   *Lesson 71*

10. All machines make it easier for someone to ▨.

11. You would have the most power if you pushed against one of the handles. Which handle is that?
12. Which handle would give you the least amount of power?

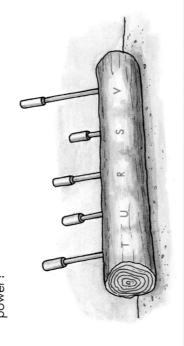

13. When people have very high fevers, how do they feel?
14. They may see and hear things that are not ▨.

Lesson 71   179

B Story Items

8. Gasoline comes from a liquid called _____

9. When Bertha first told Maria about her talent, did Maria believe her?
_____

10. How many glasses of water did Maria use to test Bertha's talent?
_____

11. **Underline** the items that tell where the water came from.
   • fish bowl   • bath tub   • jug in refrigerator   • sink
   • water heater   • frog pond   • watering can

12. Did Bertha pass Maria's test? _____

13. After the test, did Maria believe what Bertha said about her talent?
_____

14. Bertha will help Maria by telling where ▢ .
   • the oil wells are   • the water came from   • the snow was

Review Items

15. The arrow by the handle shows which way it turns. Which arrow
shows the way the log moves? _____

16. Which arrow shows the way the vine moves? _____

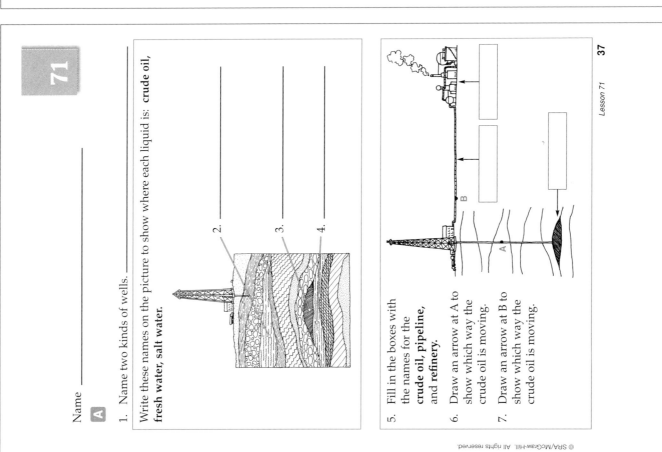

GO TO PART D IN YOUR TEXTBOOK

38   *Lesson 71*

Name _____

A

1. Name two kinds of wells. _____

Write these names on the picture to show where each liquid is: **crude oil,
fresh water, salt water.**

2. _____
3. _____
4. _____

5. Fill in the boxes with
the names for the
**crude oil, pipeline,
and refinery.**

6. Draw an arrow at A to
show which way the
crude oil is moving.

7. Draw an arrow at B to
show which way the
crude oil is moving.

Lesson 71   37

Lesson 21

EXERCISE 1
VOCABULARY

a. **Find page 352 in your textbook.** ✓
- Touch sentence 4. ✓
- This is a new vocabulary sentence. It says: The smell attracted flies immediately. Everybody, say that sentence. Get ready. (Signal.) *The smell attracted flies immediately.*
- Close your eyes and say the sentence. Get ready. (Signal.) *The smell attracted flies immediately.*
- (Repeat until firm.)

b. The smell **attracted** flies. If the smell attracted flies, the smell really interested the flies and pulled them toward the smell. Everybody, what word means **really interested** the flies? (Signal.) *Attracted.*

c. The sentence says the smell attracted flies **immediately. Immediately** means **right now.** Everybody, what word means **right now?** (Signal.) *Immediately.*

d. Listen to the sentence again: The smell attracted flies immediately. Everybody, say that sentence. Get ready. (Signal.) *The smell attracted flies immediately.*

e. What word means **really interested** the flies? (Signal.) *Attracted.*
- What word means **right now?** (Signal.) *Immediately.*

EXERCISE 2
READING WORDS

Column 1

a. Find lesson 21 in your textbook. ✓
- Touch column 1. ✓
- (Teacher reference:)

1. mukluks	3. hailstone
2. wrist	4. playfully

b. Word 1 is **mukluks.** What word? (Signal.) *Mukluks.*
- Spell **mukluks.** Get ready. (Tap for each letter.) *M-U-K-L-U-K-S.*
- Mukluks are very warm boots that Eskimos wear.

c. Word 2 is **wrist.** What word? (Signal.) *Wrist.*
- Spell **wrist.** Get ready. (Tap for each letter.) *W-R-I-S-T.*
- Your wrist is the joint between your hand and your arm. Everybody, touch your wrist. ✓

d. Word 3. What word? (Signal.) *Hailstone.*

e. Word 4. What word? (Signal.) *Playfully.*

f. Let's read those words again, the fast way.
- Word 1. What word? (Signal.) *Mukluks.*
- (Repeat for words 2–4.)

g. (Repeat step f until firm.)

Column 2

h. Find column 2. ✓
- (Teacher reference:)

1. gulped	4. wavy
2. gently	5. kneeled
3. owed	6. dents

i. All these words have an ending.

j. Word 1. What word? (Signal.) *Gulped.*
- When you gulp something, you swallow it quickly. Here's another way of saying **She swallowed the water quickly: She gulped the water.**
- What's another way of saying **They swallowed their food quickly?** (Signal.) *They gulped their food.*
- Word 2. What word? (Signal.) *Gently.*
- Things that are gentle are the opposite of things that are rough. Everybody, what's the opposite of **a rough touch?** (Signal.) *A gentle touch.*
- What's the opposite of someone who behaves roughly? (Signal.) *Someone who behaves gently.*
- (Repeat until firm.)
- Word 3. What word? (Signal.) *Owed.*
- Something that you owe is something that you must pay. If you owe five dollars, you must pay five dollars. If you owe somebody a favor, you must pay that person a favor.

• Word 4. What word? (Signal.) *Wavy.*
• (Repeat for: **5. kneeled, 6. dents.**)

k. Let's read those words again, the fast way.
• Word 1. What word? (Signal.) *Gulped.*
• (Repeat for: **2. gently, 3. owed, 4. wavy, 5. kneeled, 6. dents.**)
l. (Repeat step k until firm.)

Column 3

m. Find column 3. ✓
• (Teacher reference:)

1. rose	**3. marble**
2. sight	**4. dove**

n. Word 1. What word? (Signal.) *Rose.*
• Something that moves up today rises. Something that moved up yesterday **rose.** Everybody, what do we say for something that moves up today? (Signal.) *Rises.*
• What do we say for something that moved up yesterday? (Signal.) *Rose.*
• Word 2. What word? *Sight.*
• A sight is something you see. A terrible sight is something terrible that you see. Everybody, what do we call something **wonderful** that you see? (Signal.) *A wonderful sight.*
• Word 3. What word? (Signal.) *Marble.*
• Word 4 rhymes with **stove.** What word? (Signal.) *Dove.*

o. Let's read those words again.
• Word 1. What word? (Signal.) *Rose.*
• (Repeat for words 2–4.)
p. (Repeat step o until firm.)

Individual Turns

(For columns 1–3: Call on individual students, each to read one to three words per turn.)

EXERCISE 3

COMPREHENSION PASSAGE

a. Find part B in your textbook. ✓
• You're going to read the next story about Oomoo and Oolak. First, you'll read the information passage. It gives some facts about clouds.
b. Everybody, touch the title. ✓
• (Call on a student to read the title.) *[Facts About Clouds.]*

• Everybody, what's the title? (Signal.) *Facts About Clouds.*
c. (Call on individual students to read the passage, each student reading two or three sentences at a time. Ask the specified questions as the students read.)

> **Facts About Clouds**
> **You have read about a big storm cloud. Here are facts about clouds:**
> **Clouds are made up of tiny drops of water.**

• Everybody, say that fact. Get ready. (Signal.) *Clouds are made up of tiny drops of water.*

> **In clouds that are very high, the water drops are frozen. Here is how those clouds look.**

Picture 1   Picture 2

• Everybody, in what kind of clouds are the water drops frozen? (Signal.) *In clouds that are very high.*
• Touch a high cloud. ✓
• Those clouds are very pretty in the sunlight because the light bounces off the tiny frozen drops.

> **Some kinds of clouds may bring days of bad weather. These are low, flat clouds that look like bumpy blankets.**

• Everybody, what kind of clouds may bring days of bad weather? (Signal.) *Low, flat clouds.*
• Does that kind of cloud pass over quickly? (Signal.) *No.*
• Touch a low, flat cloud. ✓
• How long may that kind of cloud be around? (Call on a student. Idea: *Days.*)

> **Some clouds are storm clouds. They are flat on the bottom, but they go up very high. Sometimes they are five miles high.**

118 *Lesson 21*

- Tell me how a storm cloud looks. (Call on a student. Idea: *It's flat on the bottom and it goes up very high.*)
- Everybody, how high is the top of a big storm cloud sometimes? (Signal.) *Five miles.*

> **The arrows in picture 3 show how the winds move inside a storm cloud. The winds move water drops to the top of the cloud.**

- Everybody, touch the number **1** that is inside the cloud. ✓
- That's where a drop of water starts. The wind blows it up to the top of the cloud. Everybody, follow the arrow to the top of the cloud and then stop. ✓
- Tell me about the temperature of the air at the top of the cloud. Get ready. (Signal.) *It's freezing cold.*
- So what's going to happen to the drop? (Call on a student. Idea: *It will freeze.*)

> **The drops freeze. When a drop freezes, it becomes a tiny hailstone.**

- Everybody, what do we call a drop when it moves up and freezes? (Signal.) *A tiny hailstone.*

> **The tiny hailstone falls to the bottom of the cloud.**

- Everybody, touch the number **2** in the cloud. ✓
- That's where the drop freezes. Now it falls down. Everybody, follow the arrow down. ✓
- What's the temperature like at the bottom of the cloud? (Signal.) *It's warm.*

> **At the bottom of the cloud, the tiny hailstone gets covered with more water. Then it goes up again and freezes again.**

- Everybody, when it gets to the top of the cloud, what's going to happen to the water that is covering it? (Signal.) *It will freeze.*

> **Now the hailstone is a little bigger. It keeps going around and around in the cloud until it gets so heavy that it falls from the cloud. Sometimes it is as big as a baseball. Sometimes it is smaller than a marble.**

- Everybody, touch the number **1** in the cloud. ✓
- Pretend that your finger is a drop. Show me a drop that goes around inside the cloud four times. Each time it goes through the top of the cloud, say: "It freezes." Go. ✓

> **If you want to see how many times a hailstone has gone to the top of the cloud, break the hailstone in half. You'll see rings.**

- Everybody, what will you see inside the hailstone? (Signal.) *Rings.*

> **Each ring shows one trip to the top of the cloud. Count the rings and you'll know how many times the hailstone went through the cloud. Hailstone A went through the cloud three times.**

- The rings are numbered. Everybody, count the rings in hailstone A out loud, starting with the center circle. Get ready. (Signal.) *One, two, three.*

> **How many times did Hailstone B go through the cloud?**

- Everybody, figure out the answer. Remember to count the outside ring. (Wait.)
- How many times? (Signal.) *Seven.*

EXERCISE 4
STORY READING

a. Find part C in your textbook. ✓
- The error limit for group reading is 12 errors.
b. Everybody, touch the title. ✓
- (Call on a student to read the title.) *[The Killer Whales Wait.]*
- Everybody, what's the title? (Signal.) *The Killer Whales Wait.*

- Where were Oolak and Oomoo when we left them? (Call on a student. Idea: *Floating on an ice chunk.*)
c. (Call on individual students to read the story, each student reading two or three sentences at a time. Ask the specified questions as the students read.)

- (Correct errors: Tell the word. Direct the student to reread the sentence.)
- (If the group makes more than 12 errors, direct the students to reread the story.)

The Killer Whales Wait
Oomoo took off one of her boots. She kneeled down and slammed the boot against the surface of the ice.

- Why do you think she was doing that? (Call on a student. Idea: *She was trying to make noise so someone would hear her.*)
- Why didn't she yell? (Call on a student. Ideas: *She was losing her voice; nobody could hear her.*)

The boot made a loud spanking sound. Oolak watched for a moment, then took off one of his boots and slapped it against the surface of the ice. "Maybe they'll hear this," Oomoo said. "I hope they do," she added. But she knew that it was still raining a little bit and that the rain made noise. She also knew that she and Oolak were far from shore—too far. They were more than a mile from the tent. She guessed that the sounds they made with their boots were lost in the rain and the slight breeze that was still blowing from the south.

- Everybody, did she think that the people on the shore would hear the sounds? (Signal.) *No.*
- About how far away were these people? (Signal.) *Over a mile.*
- Why didn't she think they would hear the signal? (Call on a student. Idea: *Because the wind and rain were louder than the signal.*)

From time to time, Oomoo glanced to the ocean. She hoped that she would see the killer whales moving far away. She hoped that the sound

of the boots would scare them away. But each time she looked in their direction, she saw them moving back and forth, just past the top of the C-shaped ice floe.

- How do you think that made her feel? (Call on a student. Idea: *Afraid.*)

Suddenly, Oolak tugged on Oomoo's shoulder and pointed toward the whales. His eyes were wide. He looked as if he was ready to cry. "I know," Oomoo said.

- What does she mean when she says, "I know?" (Call on a student. Idea: *She knew the whales were there.*)

Her voice was almost a whisper. "Just keep trying to signal," she said. "Maybe the people on the shore will hear us."

- Everybody, had Oolak noticed the whales before? (Signal.) *No.*
- Why did he look as if he was ready to cry? (Call on a student. Idea: *Because he was afraid of the killer whales.*)

As she pounded her boot against the surface of the ice, she stared toward the shore. She wanted to see a kayak moving silently through the rain. She wanted to hear the signal of a bell ringing. She wanted to . . . .

- She stopped thinking about those things. I wonder why.

Suddenly, she saw something white moving through the water.

- What do you think it is? (Call on individual students. Ideas: *Another ice chunk; a boat; an animal;* etc.)

At first, she thought that it was a chunk of ice. But no, it couldn't be. It was not moving the way ice moves. It was very hard to tell what it was through the light rain. It wasn't a kayak. It wasn't a long boat. It was . . . Usk.

Usk ✦ was swimming directly toward the ice chunk. And he was moving very fast.

"Usk!" Oomoo yelled as loudly as she could. "Usk!" She stood up and waved her arms.

The huge polar bear caught up to the ice chunk when it was not more than a hundred meters away from the killer whales. "Will they go after Usk?" Oolak asked.

- Everybody, who does he think might go after Usk? (Signal.) *The killer whales.*
- How close are they to the whales now? (Call on a student. Idea: *About 100 meters.*)

"They'll go after Usk if they're hungry," Oomoo replied. "We've got to get out of here fast."

The huge bear swam up to the ice chunk, put his huge paws on the surface, and started to climb onto it. When he tried that, he almost tipped it over.

- Why? (Call on a student. Idea: *Because he was so heavy.*)

"No," Oomoo said. "Stay down." She tried to push him back. He rolled into the water and made a playful circle. "Give me your laces," Oomoo said to Oolak. Oomoo and Oolak untied the laces from their boots. These laces were long, thick straps of animal skin. Oomoo tied all the laces together. Quickly, she glanced back. The ice chunk was less than a hundred meters from the killer whales.

She called Usk. He playfully swam around the ice chunk, rolling over on his back and slapping the water with his front paws.

- What does Usk want to do? (Call on a student. Idea: *Play.*)

Oomoo waited until Usk got close to the shore side of the ice chunk.

- Everybody, which side did he move to? (Signal.) *The shore side.*

- What do you think Oomoo's going to do? (Call on a student. Idea: *Get Usk to help them get back to shore.*)

Then she slipped the laces around his neck. "Hang on tight," she told Oolak, and handed him one end of the laces. She and Oolak sat down on the ice chunk and tried to dig their heels into dents in the surface of the ice.

"Play sled," she told Usk. "Play sled. Go home."

- Read the rest of the story to yourself. Find out two things. Find out what Usk did at first. Find out something he may have seen that made him stop being playful. Raise your hand when you're done.

At first, Usk just rolled over and almost got the laces tangled in his front paws. "Home," Oomoo repeated. "Play sled and go home."

Usk stayed next to the ice chunk, making a playful sound. "Home," Oomoo shouted again.

Then Usk seemed to figure out what he was supposed to do. Perhaps he saw the fins of the killer whales. He got low in the water and started to swim toward shore.

- (After all students have raised their hands:)
- What did Oomoo keep telling Usk to do? (Call on a student. Ideas: *Go home; play sled.*)
- Everybody, did Usk do that at first? (Signal.) *No.*
- What did he do? (Call on a student. Idea: *Rolled over.*)
- What may Usk have seen that made him stop being playful? (Call on a student. Idea: *The fins of the killer whales.*)
- What did Usk do then? (Call on a student. Idea: *Swam toward shore.*)
- Everybody, look at the picture. What are Oomoo and Oolak hanging on to? (Signal.) *The laces.*
- Point on the picture to show the direction Usk is moving. ✓

EXERCISE 5
PAIRED PRACTICE

You're going to read aloud to your partner. Today the **B** members will read first. Then the **A** members will read from the star to the end of the story.
(Observe students and give feedback.)

End-of-Lesson Activities

INDEPENDENT WORK

Now finish your independent work for lesson 21. Raise your hand when you're finished. (Observe students and give feedback.)

WORKCHECK

a. (Direct students to take out their marking pencils.)
- We're going to check your independent work. Remember, if you got an item wrong, make an **X** next to the item. Don't change any answers.

b. (For each item: Read the item. Call on a student to answer it. If the answer is wrong, say the correct answer. Refer to the Answer Key for the correct answers.)
c. Now use your marking pencil to fix up any items you got wrong. Remember, all mistakes must be fixed up before you hand in your independent work.

LANGUAGE ARTS

(Present Language Arts lesson 21 after completing Reading lesson 21. See Language Arts Guide.)

ACTIVITIES

(Present Activity 2 after completing Reading lessons 21. See Activities Across the Curriculum.)

> **Note:** A special project occurs after lesson 22. See page 128 for the materials you'll need.

The *Language Arts Guide* and *Activities across the Curriculum* are not core components of *Reading Mastery* Classic.

VOCABULARY SENTENCES

Lessons 1–70

1. The horses became restless on the dangerous route.

2. Scientists do not ignore ordinary things.

3. She actually repeated that careless mistake.

4. The smell attracted flies immediately.

5. The rim of the volcano exploded.

6. The new exhibit displayed mysterious fish.

7. She automatically arranged the flowers.

8. They were impressed by her large vocabulary.

9. He responded to her clever solution.

10. The patent attorney wrote an agreement.

11. The applause interrupted his speech.

12. She selected a comfortable seat.

13. Without gravity, they were weightless.

14. She demonstrated how animals use oxygen.

15. Lava erupted from the volcano's crater.

16. The incredible whales made them anxious.

17. The boring speaker disturbed the audience.

The arrows in picture 3 show how the winds move inside a storm cloud. The winds move water drops to the top of the cloud. The drops freeze. When a drop freezes, it becomes a tiny hailstone. The tiny hailstone falls to the bottom of the cloud. At the bottom of the cloud, the tiny hailstone gets covered with more water. Then it goes up again and freezes again. Now the hailstone is a little bigger. It keeps going around and around in the cloud until it gets so heavy that it

falls from the cloud. Sometimes it is as big as a baseball. Sometimes it is smaller than a marble.

If you want to see how many times a hailstone has gone to the top of the cloud, break the hailstone in half. You'll see rings. Each ring shows one trip to the top of the cloud. Count the rings and you'll know how many times the hailstone went through the cloud. Hailstone A went through the cloud three times.

How many times did Hailstone B go through the cloud?

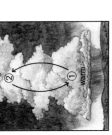

Hailstone A   Hailstone B

The Killer Whales Wait

Oomoo took off one of her boots. She kneeled down and slammed the boot against the surface of the ice. The boot made a loud spanking sound. Oolak watched for a moment, then took off one of his boots and slapped it against the surface of the ice. "Maybe they'll hear this," Oomoo said. "I hope they do," she added. But she knew that it was still raining a little bit and that the rain

made noise. She also knew that she and Oolak were far from shore—too far. They were more than a mile from the tent. She guessed that the sounds they made with their boots were lost in the rain and the slight breeze that was still blowing from the south.

From time to time, Oomoo glanced at the ocean. She hoped that she would see the killer whales

Lesson 21   105

21

1
1. mukluks
2. wrist
3. hailstone
4. playfully

2
1. gulped
2. gently
3. owed
4. wavy
5. kneeled
6. dents

3
1. rose
2. sight
3. marble
4. dove

Facts About Clouds

You have read about a big storm cloud. Here are facts about clouds:

• Clouds are made up of tiny drops of water

• In clouds that are very high, the water drops are frozen. Here is how those clouds look.

Picture 1

• Some kinds of clouds may bring days of bad weather. These are low, flat clouds that look like bumpy blankets.

Picture 2

• Some clouds are storm clouds. They are flat on the bottom, but they go up very high. Sometimes they are five miles high.

freezing cold

② ①

warm

Picture 3

104   *Lesson 21*

Reading Mastery Level 4   Textbook

moving far away. She hoped that the sound of the boots would scare them away. But each time she looked in their direction, she saw them moving back and forth, just past the top of the C-shaped ice floe.

Suddenly, Oolak tugged on Oomoo's shoulder and pointed toward the whales. His eyes were wide. He looked as if he was ready to cry. "I know," Oomoo said. "Just keep trying to signal," she said.

"Maybe the people on the shore will hear us."

As she pounded her boot against the surface of the ice, she stared toward the shore. She wanted to see a kayak moving silently through the rain. She wanted to hear the signal of a bell ringing. She wanted to . . . .

Suddenly, she saw something white moving through the water. At first, she thought that it was a chunk of ice. But no, it couldn't be. It was not moving the way ice moves. It was very hard to tell what it was through the light rain. It wasn't a kayak. It wasn't a long boat. It was . . . Usk.

Usk  was swimming directly toward the ice chunk. And he was moving very fast.

"Usk!" Oomoo yelled as loudly as she could. "Usk!" She stood up and waved her arms.

The huge polar bear caught up to the ice chunk when it was not more than a hundred meters away from the killer whales. "Will they go after Usk?" Oolak asked.

"They'll go after Usk if they're hungry," Oomoo replied. "We've got to get out of here fast."

The huge bear swam up to the ice chunk, put his huge paws on the surface, and started to climb onto it. When he tried that, he almost tipped it over.

"No," Oomoo said. "Stay down." She tried to push him back. He rolled into the water and made a playful circle. "Give me your laces," Oomoo said to Oolak. Oomoo and Oolak untied the laces from their boots. These laces were long, thick straps of animal skin. Oomoo tied all the laces together. Quickly, she glanced back. The ice chunk was less than a hundred meters from the killer whales.

She called Usk. He playfully swam around the ice chunk, rolling over on his back and slapping the water with his front paws. Oomoo waited until Usk got close to the shore side of the ice chunk. Then she slipped the laces around his neck. "Hang on tight," she told Oolak, and handed him one end of the laces. She and Oolak sat down on the ice chunk and tried to dig

their heels into dents in the surface of the ice.

"Play sled," she told Usk. "Play sled. Go home."

At first, Usk just rolled over and almost got the laces tangled in his front paws. "Home," Oomoo repeated. "Play sled and go home."

Usk stayed next to the ice chunk, making a playful sound. "Home," Oomoo shouted again.

Then Usk seemed to figure out what he was supposed to do. Perhaps he saw the fins of the killer whales. He got low in the water and started to swim toward shore.

D Number your paper from 1 through 12.

Story Items

1. What were Oomoo's boot laces made of?
2. What did Oomoo do with the laces after she tied them together?
3. What did she want Usk to do?
4. Did Usk immediately understand what he was supposed to do?
5. What did Usk start doing at the end of the story?

Review Items

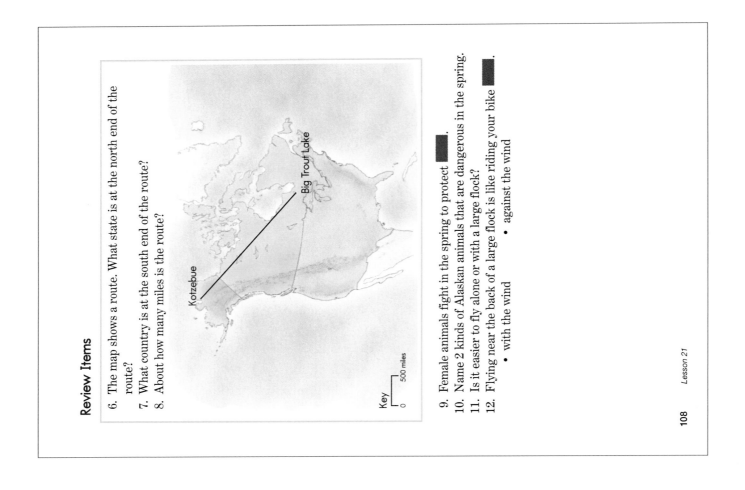

Kotzebue

Big Trout Lake

Key
0   500 miles

6. The map shows a route. What state is at the north end of the route?
7. What country is at the south end of the route?
8. About how many miles is the route?

9. Female animals fight in the spring to protect ▉.
10. Name 2 kinds of Alaskan animals that are dangerous in the spring.
11. Is it easier to fly alone or with a large flock?
12. Flying near the back of a large flock is like riding your bike ▉.
   • with the wind   • against the wind

Lesson 21

108

B   Story Items

12. Oomoo slapped her boot on the ice to make noise. Why did she want the people on shore to hear the noise? _____

13. Why did she want the killer whales to hear the noise? _____

14. Was Oomoo sure that someone would hear her? _____

15. About how far was the ice chunk from the tent? _____

16. About how far was the ice chunk from the killer whales? _____

Review Items

17. Write **north**, **south**, **east** and **west** in the correct boxes.

18. In which direction is ocean current **J** moving? _____

19. In which direction is ocean current **K** moving? _____

20. Which direction is the wind coming from? _____

21. Make an arrow above ice chunk **L** to show the direction the current will move the ice chunk.

22. Make an arrow above ice chunk **M** to show the direction the current will move the ice chunk.

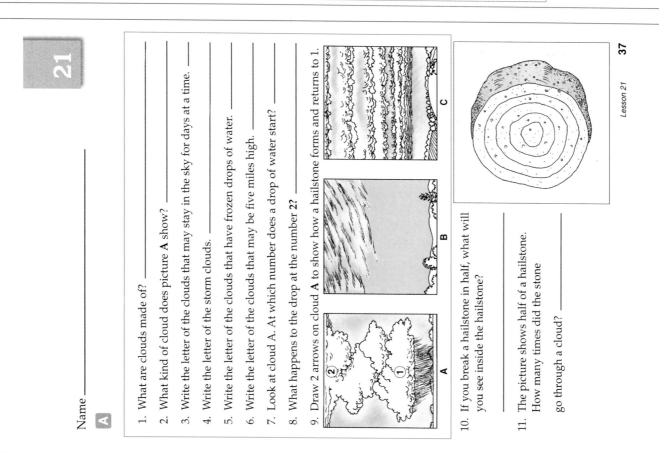

GO TO PART D IN YOUR TEXTBOOK.

38   *Lesson 21*

Name _____

21

A

1. What are clouds made of? _____

2. What kind of cloud does picture **A** show? _____

3. Write the letter of the clouds that may stay in the sky for days at a time. _____

4. Write the letter of the storm clouds. _____

5. Write the letter of the clouds that have frozen drops of water. _____

6. Write the letter of the clouds that may be five miles high. _____

7. Look at cloud **A**. At which number does a drop of water start? _____

8. What happens to the drop at the number **2**? _____

9. Draw 2 arrows on cloud **A** to show how a hailstone forms and returns to 1.

10. If you break a hailstone in half, what will you see inside the hailstone? _____

11. The picture shows half of a hailstone. How many times did the stone go through a cloud? _____

Lesson 21   **37**

Lesson 76

BEFORE READING

Have students find lesson 76, part A, in their textbooks.

HARD WORDS

1. Everybody, find column 1. ✓
   - The words in this column are hard words from your textbook stories.

1. soothe	5. conceal
2. persuade	6. dread
3. pirates	7. hasty
4. poverty	

2. Word 1 is **soothe.** Everybody, what word? (Signal.) *Soothe.*
   - (Repeat for every word in the column.)
3. Let's read these words again.
4. Word 1. Everybody, what word? (Signal.) *Soothe.*
   - (Repeat for every word in the column.)
5. (Repeat the column until firm.)

COMPOUND WORDS

1. Everybody, find column 2. ✓
   - All these compound words consist of two short words.

1. shipwreck	4. halfway
2. horseback	5. courtyard
3. anybody	6. folktale

2. Word 1. Everybody, what's the first short word? (Signal.) *Ship.*
   - Everybody, what's the compound word? (Signal.) *Shipwreck.*
   - (Repeat for every word in the column.)
3. (Repeat the column until firm.)

WORD PRACTICE

1. Everybody, find column 3. ✓
   - We're going to practice these words.

1. ridicule	5. excuses
2. Beauty	6. ridiculed
3. cautious	7. countries
4. fatigue	8. furniture

2. Word 1. Everybody, what word? (Signal.) *Ridicule.*
   - (Repeat for every word in the column.)
3. (Repeat the column until firm.)

VOCABULARY REVIEW

1. Everybody, find column 4. ✓
   - You've learned the meaning for all these words.

1. vanish	5. dimple
2. original	6. greedy
3. insane	7. victim
4. glossy	

2. Word 1. Everybody, what word? (Signal.) *Vanish.*
   - (Repeat for every word in the column.)
3. (Repeat the column until firm.)
4. Now let's talk about what the words mean.

Word 1

1. Word 1 is **vanish.**
   - What does **vanish** mean? (Idea: *Disappear.*)
2. Everybody, what's another way of saying **The mysterious stranger disappeared**? (Signal.) *The mysterious stranger vanished.*

Word 2

1. Word 2 is **original.**
   - What is an **original**? (Idea: *Something that is not a copy of anything else.*)

Lesson 76 **77**

Word 3
1. Word 3 is **insane**.
   - What does **insane** mean? (Idea: *Crazy.*)
2. Everybody, what's another way of saying **He had a crazy desire for wealth**? (Signal.) *He had an insane desire for wealth.*

Word 4
1. Word 4 is **glossy**.
   - What does **glossy** mean? (Idea: *Smooth and shiny.*)

Word 5
1. Word 5 is **dimple**.
   - What is a **dimple**? (Idea: *A little dent in your cheek or chin.*)

Word 6
1. Word 6 is **greedy**.
   - What does **greedy** mean? (Idea: *You are never satisfied with what you have.*)

Word 7
1. Word 7 is **victim**.
   - What is a **victim**? (Idea: *A person who is harmed.*)

EXERCISE 5
VOCABULARY PREVIEW
1. Everybody, find column 5. ✓
   - First we'll read the words in this column. Then we'll read the words in sentences.

1. desolate	4. selfish
2. persuade	5. soothe
3. terrify	6. poverty

2. Word 1. Everybody, what word? (Signal.) *Desolate.*
   - (Repeat for every word in the column.)
3. (Repeat the column until firm.)

EXERCISE 6
VOCABULARY FROM CONTEXT
1. Everybody, find part B. ✓
   - These sentences use the words you just read.
2. We're going to use the rest of the sentence to figure out the meaning of the word in bold type.

Sentence 1
1. There was nothing within a hundred miles of this lonely, **desolate** place.

1. (Call on a student to read the sentence.)
   - What could **desolate** mean? (Ideas: *Gloomy; barren; uninhabited.*)

Sentence 2
2. She was good at talking people into doing things, but she could not **persuade** anybody to go to the beach with her.

1. (Call on a student to read the sentence.)
   - What could **persuade** mean? (Idea: *Convince.*)

Sentence 3
3. The old house was frightening, and the sounds within it **terrified** me.

1. (Call on a student to read the sentence.)
   - What could **terrified** mean? (Idea: *Greatly frightened.*)

Sentence 4
4. She seemed to be kind, but she was really very **selfish** and thought of nobody but herself.

1. (Call on a student to read the sentence.)
   - What could **selfish** mean? (Idea: *Concerned only with herself.*)

Sentence 5
5. He was so upset that nothing we could do would comfort or **soothe** him.

1. (Call on a student to read the sentence.)
   - What could **soothe** mean? (Ideas: *Relax; make him feel better.*)

Sentence 6
6. At first he was wealthy, but then he lost all his wealth and found himself in **poverty**.

1. (Call on a student to read the sentence.)
   - What could **poverty** mean? (Ideas: *Without money; the state of being poor.*)

READING

STORY BACKGROUND

1. Everybody, find part C. ✓
2. (Call on individual students to read two or three sentences each.)
3. (After students complete each section, ask the questions for that section.)

Folktales

The next story you will read is a folktale called "Beauty and the Beast." Like myths, folktales are old stories that people told aloud before someone wrote them down. But folktales are usually much newer than myths. The myths you have just read, for example, take place about three thousand years ago. In comparison, "Beauty and the Beast" takes place just a few hundred years ago.

Another difference is that myths usually include gods and goddesses, but folktales do not. Instead, folktales often have witches, wizards, or other kinds of magic.

• Who were the gods in the myths you have read? (Ideas: *Zeus, Hermes; the stranger in "The Golden Touch."*)
• Who can name some folktales that have witches or wizards? (Ideas: *Cinderella; Sleeping Beauty; Snow White; Hansel and Gretel.*)

"Beauty and the Beast" is one of the most famous folktales of all time. Many movies have been made of the story, and many writers have retold it in their own words. The story comes from France, a large country in Europe.

• How many of you have seen a movie of "Beauty and the Beast"? (Have students raise their hands.)
• The version you will read is different from the movie versions.

READING ALOUD

1. Everybody, find part D. ✓
• The error limit for this lesson is 10.
2. (Call on individual students to read two or three sentences each.)

3. (After students complete each section, ask the questions for that section.)

Beauty and the Beast
Chapter 1

Once upon a time there lived a merchant who was enormously rich. The merchant had six sons and six daughters, and he would let them have anything they wanted.

• What do merchants do? (Idea: *Buy and sell things.*)
• How many children did the merchant have in all? (Response: *Twelve.*)
• How do you think those children might behave if they got everything they wanted? (Ideas: *They might be spoiled; they might be ungrateful.*)

But one day their house caught fire and burned to the ground, with all the splendid furniture, books, pictures, gold, silver, and precious goods it contained. Yet this was only the beginning of their misfortune. Shortly after the fire, the merchant lost every ship he had upon the sea, either because of pirates, shipwrecks, or fire. Then he heard that the people who worked for him in distant countries had stolen his money. At last, he fell into great poverty.

• Name some things that went wrong for the merchant. (Ideas: *His house burned down; he lost all his ships; the people who worked for him stole his money.*)
• How rich was the merchant after all this misfortune? (Ideas: *He wasn't rich; he was poor.*)

All the merchant had after those misfortunes was a little cottage in a desolate place a hundred miles from the town in which he used to live. He moved into the cottage with his children. They were in despair at the idea of leading such a different life. The cottage stood in the middle of a dark forest, and it seemed to be the most dismal place on earth. The children had to cultivate the fields to earn their living. They were poorly clothed, and they missed the comforts and amusements of their earlier life. Only the youngest daughter tried to be brave and cheerful. She had also been sad at first, but she soon recovered her good nature. She set to work to make the best of things. But when she tried to persuade her sisters to join her in dancing and singing, they ridiculed her and said that this miserable life was all she was fit for. But she was far prettier and more clever than they were. She was so lovely that she was called Beauty.

- Why do you think working was especially hard for these children? (Idea: *Because they were used to having servants do all the work.*)
- What's the title of this story? (Response: *Beauty and the Beast.*)
- Who do you think one of the main characters will be? (Response: *Beauty.*)
- Who will the other main character be? (Response: *The Beast.*)

After two years, their father received news that one of his ships, which he had believed to be lost, had come safely into port with a rich cargo. All the sons and daughters at once thought their poverty would be over, and they wanted to set out directly for the town. But their father was more cautious, so he decided to go by himself. Only Beauty had any doubt that they would soon be rich again. The other daughters gave their father requests for so many jewels and dresses that it would have taken a fortune to buy them. But Beauty did not ask for anything. Her father noticed her silence and said, "And what shall I bring for you, Beauty?"

"The only thing I wish for is to see you come home safely," she answered.

This reply angered her sisters, who thought she was accusing them of asking for costly things. But her father was pleased. Still, he told her to choose something.

"Well, dear Father," she said, "since you insist upon it, I want you to bring me a rose. I have not seen one since we came here, and I love them very much." ♦

- What did Beauty's sisters ask for? (Idea: *Jewels and dresses.*)
- Why do you think Beauty asked for a rose? (Ideas: *Because she loved roses; because roses are beautiful; because roses don't cost much money.*)

80 *Lesson 76*

EXERCISE 9

SILENT READING

1. Read the rest of the chapter to yourselves and be ready to answer some questions.

So the merchant set out on horseback and reached the town as quickly as possible. But when he got there, he found out that his partners had taken the goods the ship had brought. So he found himself poorer than when he had left the cottage. He had only enough money to buy food on his journey home. To make matters worse, he left town during terrible weather. The storm was so bad that he was exhausted with cold and fatigue before he was halfway home. Night came on, and the deep snow and bitter frost made it impossible for the merchant's horse to carry him any further.

The merchant could see no houses or lights. The only shelter he could find was the hollow trunk of a great tree. He crouched there all night long. It was the longest night he had ever known. In spite of his weariness, the howling of the wolves kept him awake. And when the day broke, he was not much better off, for falling snow had covered up every path, and he did not know which way to turn.

At last, he made out some sort of path, and he started to follow it. It was rough and slippery, so he kept falling down. But the path soon became easier, and it led him to a row of trees that ended at a splendid castle. It seemed very strange to the merchant that no snow had fallen in the row of trees. Stranger still, the trees were fruit trees, and they were covered with apples and oranges. ★

The merchant walked down the row of trees and soon reached the castle. He called, but nobody answered. So he opened the door and called again. Then he climbed up a flight of steps and walked through several splendid rooms. The pleasant warmth of the air refreshed him, and he suddenly felt very hungry; but there seemed to be nobody in this huge palace who could give him anything to eat.

The merchant kept wandering through the deep silence of the splendid rooms. At last, he stopped in a room smaller than the rest, where a bright fire was burning next to a couch. The merchant thought this room must be prepared for someone, so he sat down to wait. But very soon he fell into a heavy sleep.

His extreme hunger wakened him after several hours. He was still alone, but a good dinner had been set on a little table. The merchant had eaten nothing for an entire day, so he lost no time in beginning his meal, which was delicious. He wondered who had brought the food, but no one appeared.

After dinner, the merchant went to sleep again. He woke completely refreshed the next morning. There was still no sign of anybody, although a fresh meal of cakes and fruit was sitting on the little table at his elbow. The silence began to terrify the merchant, and he decided to search once more through the rooms. But it was no use. There was no sign of life in the palace. Not even a mouse could be seen.

- What bad news did the merchant discover when he reached the town? (Idea: *His partners had taken everything off the ship.*)
- What was the weather like when he started back home? (Idea: *Cold and snowy.*)
- Why did he have trouble finding his way in the morning? (Idea: *Snow had covered up the path.*)
- What was unusual about the row of trees? (Ideas: *They had no snow on them; they had fruit on them.*)
- What was unusual about the castle? (Ideas: *Nobody was there; a fire was burning by itself; food appeared while the merchant was sleeping.*)
- Why did the merchant search through the palace the next day? (Ideas: *To see if anybody was there; to find the owner.*)
- Who do you think the castle belongs to? (Ideas: *The Beast; a witch; a wizard.*)

EXERCISE 10
PAIRED PRACTICE

1. Now you'll read in pairs.
   - Whoever read second the last time will read first today.
   - Remember to start at the diamond and switch at the star.
2. (Observe students and answer questions as needed.)

AFTER READING

EXERCISE 11
INDEPENDENT WORK

1. Do all the items in your workbook and textbook for this lesson.
2. (The independent work in this lesson includes the following activities.)
- Story details
- Vocabulary
- Sequencing
- Related facts
- Story review
- Main idea
- Comprehension
- Writing

EXERCISE 12
WORKCHECK

1. (Using the Answer Key, read the questions and answers for the workbook.)
2. (Have students read their answers for the textbook activities.)
3. (Have two or three students read their writing assignments aloud. Comment on each assignment.)
4. (Have students correct and turn in their work.)

LANGUAGE ARTS GUIDE

(Students should complete the appropriate exercises in the *Language Arts Guide* after completing lesson 76. See *Language Arts Guide* for details.)

The *Language Arts Guide* is not a core component of *Reading Mastery* Classic.

Lesson 76   **81**

76

A WORD LISTS

1
Hard Words
1. soothe
2. persuade
3. pirates
4. poverty
5. conceal
6. dread
7. hasty

2
Compound Words
1. shipwreck
2. horseback
3. anybody
4. halfway
5. courtyard
6. folktale

3
Word Practice
1. ridicule
2. Beauty
3. cautious
4. fatigue
5. excuses
6. ridiculed
7. countries
8. furniture

4
Vocabulary Review
1. vanish
2. original
3. insane
4. glossy
5. dimple
6. greedy
7. victim

5
Vocabulary Preview
1. desolate
2. persuade
3. terrify
4. selfish
5. soothe
6. poverty

B VOCABULARY FROM CONTEXT

1. There was nothing within a hundred miles of this lonely, **desolate** place.
2. She was good at talking people into doing things, but she could not **persuade** anybody to go to the beach with her.
3. The old house was frightening, and the sounds within it **terrified** me.
4. She seemed to be kind, but she was really very **selfish** and thought of nobody but herself.
5. He was so upset that nothing we could do would comfort or **soothe** him.
6. At first he was wealthy, but then he lost all his wealth and found himself in **poverty.**

C STORY BACKGROUND

Folktales

The next story you will read is a folktale called "Beauty and the Beast." Like myths, folktales are old stories that people told aloud before someone wrote them down. But folktales are usually much newer than myths. The myths you have just read, for example, take place about three thousand years ago. In comparison, "Beauty and the Beast" takes place just a few hundred years ago.

Another difference is that myths usually include gods and goddesses, but folktales do not. Instead, folktales often have witches, wizards, or other kinds of magic.

"Beauty and the Beast" is one of the most famous folktales of all time. Many movies have been made of the story, and many writers have retold it in their own words. The story comes from France, a large country in Europe.

D READING

Beauty and the Beast
Chapter 1

Once upon a time there lived a merchant who was enormously rich. The merchant had six sons and six daughters, and he would let them have anything they wanted.

But one day their house caught fire and burned to the ground, with all the splendid furniture, books, pictures, gold, silver, and precious goods it contained. Yet this was only the beginning of their misfortune. Shortly after the fire, the merchant lost every ship he had upon the sea, either because of pirates, shipwrecks, or fire. Then he heard that the people who worked for him in distant countries had stolen his money. At last, he fell into great poverty.

All the merchant had after those misfortunes was a little cottage in a desolate place a hundred miles from the town in which he used to live. He moved into the cottage with his children. They were in despair at the idea of leading such a different life. The cottage stood in the middle of a dark forest, and it seemed to be the most dismal place on earth.

The children had to cultivate the fields to earn their living. They were poorly clothed, and they missed the comforts and amusements of their earlier life. Only the youngest daughter tried to be brave and cheerful. She had also been sad at first, but she soon recovered her good nature. She set to work to make the best of things. But when she tried to persuade her sisters to join her in dancing and singing, they ridiculed her and said that this miserable life was all she was fit for. But she was far prettier and more clever than they were. She was so lovely that she was called Beauty.

After two years, their father received news that one of his ships, which he had believed to be lost, had come safely into port with a rich cargo. All the sons and daughters at once thought their poverty would be over, and they wanted to set out directly for the town. But their father was more cautious, so he decided to go by himself. Only Beauty had any doubt that they would soon be rich again. The other daughters gave their father requests for so many jewels and dresses that it would have taken a fortune to buy them. But Beauty did not ask for anything. Her father noticed her silence and said, "And what shall I bring for you, Beauty?"

"The only thing I wish for is to see you come home safely," she answered.

This reply angered her sisters, who thought she was accusing them of asking for costly things. But her father was pleased. Still, he told her to choose something.

"Well, dear Father," she said, "since you insist upon it, I want you to bring me a rose. I have not seen one since we came here, and I love them very much." ◆

So the merchant set out on horseback and reached the town as quickly as possible. But when he got there, he found out that his partners had taken the goods the ship had brought. So he found himself poorer than when he had left the cottage. He had only enough money to buy food on his journey home. To make matters worse, he left town during terrible weather. The storm was so bad that he was exhausted with cold and fatigue before he was halfway home. Night came on, and the deep snow and bitter frost made it impossible for the merchant's horse to carry him any further.

The merchant could see no houses or lights. The only shelter he could find was the hollow trunk of a great tree. He crouched there all night long. It was the longest night he had ever known. In spite of his weariness, the howling of the wolves kept him awake. And when the day broke, he was not much better off, for falling snow had covered up every path, and he did not know which way to turn.

At last, he made out some sort of path, and he started to follow it. It was rough and slippery, so he kept falling down. But the path soon became easier, and it led him to a row of trees that ended at a splendid castle. It seemed very strange to the merchant that no snow had fallen in the row of trees. Stranger still, the trees were fruit trees, and they were covered with apples and oranges. ★

The merchant walked down the row of trees and soon reached the castle. He called, but nobody answered. So he opened the door and called again. Then he climbed

Lesson 76   77

up a flight of steps and walked through several splendid rooms. The pleasant warmth of the air refreshed him, and he suddenly felt very hungry; but there seemed to be nobody in this huge palace who could give him anything to eat.

a good dinner had been set on a little table. The merchant had eaten nothing for an entire day, so he lost no time in beginning his meal, which was delicious. He wondered who had brought the food, but no one appeared.

The merchant kept wandering through the deep silence of the splendid rooms. At last, he stopped in a room smaller than the rest, where a bright fire was burning next to a couch. The merchant thought this room must be prepared for someone, so he sat down to wait. But very soon he fell into a heavy sleep.

His extreme hunger wakened him after several hours. He was still alone, but

After dinner, the merchant went to sleep again. He woke completely refreshed the next morning. There was still no sign of anybody, although a fresh meal of cakes and fruit was sitting on the little table at his elbow. The silence began to terrify the merchant, and he decided to search once more through the rooms. But it was no use. There was no sign of life in the palace. Not even a mouse could be seen.

78   *Lesson 76*

E MAIN IDEA

For each paragraph, write a sentence that tells the complete main idea.

1. Saturday finally arrived. Janet took her camera out of her closet. Then she went outside to look for her friends. When she had found everybody, she told them to stand together on her porch. She looked through her camera and told everybody to stand closer together. Finally, she said, "Smile," and pressed the button on the camera. The camera went "click," and some of Janet's friends made faces.

2. William liked rowing boats. Last spring, William visited Swan Lake. He rented a rowboat for the whole day. He hopped into the boat and started to pull the oars. The boat started across the lake. William could see the boat rental place getting farther and farther away. William kept rowing. He looked at people fishing and at birds flying near the water. He had fun seeing how fast he could row. After a long time, he came to the opposite side of the lake.

F COMPREHENSION

Write the answers.
1. Why were most of the merchant's children greedy and spoiled?
2. Name at least three ways that Beauty was different from her sisters.
3. Why do you think Beauty asked her father for a rose?
4. Why did the merchant get lost on the way home?
5. Name at least three strange things about the palace.

G WRITING

What objects do you think are beautiful?
• Pick an object that you think is beautiful, such as a flower, a painting, or a river. Then write a poem about the object. Describe what the object looks like and tell why you think it's beautiful.

76

Name _____

A STORY DETAILS

Write the answers.

1. At the beginning of the story, how rich was the merchant?

_____

2. How many children did the merchant have?

_____

3. What happened to his house?

_____

4. What kind of house did the family move into?

_____

5. Before her father left for town, what did Beauty ask him to bring back?

_____

6. What kinds of things did the other children ask for?

_____

7. Where did the merchant sleep during the storm?

_____

8. What was strange about the row of trees the merchant found?

_____

9. Why was the palace so silent?

_____

B VOCABULARY

Write the correct words in the blanks.

shrewd	calculate
witty	century
appetite	secure
inhabitant	sympathy
discontented	defeat

1. Lillian was so _____ with her job that she quit.

2. The wise man made many _____ decisions.

3. A _____ is a long time.

4. The experts could not _____ the number of stars in the sky.

5. She was glad to see the food because she had an enormous _____.

6. The cat was _____ from dogs as long as it stayed inside the house.

7. After the child fell, her mother held her and showed great _____.

C SEQUENCING

Put the following events in the correct order by numbering them from **1** to **5**.

____ The merchant found a palace.

____ The merchant spent the night in a tree.

____ The merchant moved to a cottage.

____ The merchant's house burned down.

____ The merchant went back to the town.

D RELATED FACTS

Write which Greek god each statement describes. Choose **Hermes, Poseidon,** or **Zeus.**

1. The god of the sky

_____

2. The god of the ocean

_____

3. The god of travelers

_____

E STORY REVIEW

Write whether each statement describes **The Miraculous Pitcher** or **The Golden Touch.**

1. Zeus appeared in this story.

_____

2. The main character was a king.

_____

3. One of the characters had a magic staff.

_____

4. One of the characters was changed into a statue.

_____

5. The story showed how evil greed can be.

_____

6. The story showed why you should be kind to strangers.

_____

■ GO TO PART E IN YOUR TEXTBOOK. ■

Lesson 57

BEFORE READING

Have students find lesson 57, part A, in their textbooks.

EXERCISE 1
HARD WORDS

1. Look at column 1.
   • These are hard words from your textbook stories.

1. heron	4. wilderness
2. trio	5. gallant
3. Sylvia	6. pigeon

2. Word 1 is **heron**. Everybody, what word? (Signal.) *Heron.*
   • (Repeat this procedure for every word in the column.)
3. Let's read the words again.
4. Word 1. Everybody, what word? (Signal.) *Heron.*
   • (Repeat this procedure for every word in the column.)
5. (Repeat the column until firm.)

EXERCISE 2
WORD PRACTICE

1. Look at column 2.
   • We're going to practice these words.

1. Circe	3. Scylla
2. Calypso	

2. Word 1. Everybody, what word? (Signal.) *Circe.*
   • (Repeat this procedure for every word in the column.)
3. (Repeat the column until firm.)

EXERCISE 3
NEW VOCABULARY

1. Look at column 3.
   • First we'll read the words in this column. Then we'll read their definitions.

1. heron	5. gallant
2. foster parent	6. trio
3. huckleberry	7. game
4. bough	

2. Word 1. Everybody, what word? (Signal.) *Heron.*
   • (Repeat this procedure for every word in the column.)
3. (Repeat the column until firm.)

EXERCISE 4
VOCABULARY DEFINITIONS

1. Everybody, find part B. ✓
   • These are definitions for the words you just read.
2. (For each word, call on a student to read the definition and the item. Then ask the student to complete the item.)

1. **heron**—*Herons* are birds that wade through water and eat frogs and fish. Herons usually have tall, thin legs and a long, S-shaped neck. The picture shows a *white heron.*
   • Describe a heron.
   • What's the answer? (Ideas: *It has tall, thin legs and a long, S-shaped neck; it wades through water and eats frogs and fish.*)

2. **foster parent**—A *foster parent* is somebody who brings up a child but is not the child's real parent.
   • What do we call somebody who brings up a child but is not the child's real parent?
   • What's the answer? (Response: *A foster parent.*)

3. **huckleberry**—A *huckleberry* is a small purple or black berry that grows on bushes.
   • What is a huckleberry?
   • What's the answer? (Idea: *A small purple or black berry that grows on bushes.*)

4. **bough**—A *bough* of a tree is a branch of the tree.
   • What is a branch of a tree?

• What's the answer? (Response: *A bough*.)

5. **gallant**—Somebody who is *gallant* is brave and noble.
   • What's another way of saying *He was a noble warrior*?

• What's the answer? (Response: *He was a gallant warrior*.)

6. **trio**—A *trio* is a group of three.
   • What's another way of saying *A group of three went to the river*?

• What's the answer? (Response: *A trio went to the river*.)

7. **game**—Wild animals that are hunted are called *game*.
   • What do we call wild animals that are hunted?

• What's the answer? (Response: *Game*.)

EXERCISE 5

INFERENCE

1. Everybody, turn to part D at the end of today's story. ✓
• (Call on individual students to read several sentences each.)
• (At the end of each section, present the questions for that section.)

Write the answers for items 1–8.
   You have to answer different types of questions about the passages you read. Some questions are answered by words in the passage. Other questions are *not* answered by words in the passage. You have to figure out the answer by making a deduction.

• What do you use to answer the first kind of question? (Idea: *Words in the passage*.)
• What do you use to answer the second kind of question? (Idea: *A deduction*.)

The following passage includes both types of questions.
More about Ecology
   Two hundred years ago, many people were not concerned with ecology. They believed there was no end to the different types of wildlife, so they killed wild animals by the hundreds of thousands. When we look back on these killings, we may feel shocked. But for the people who lived two hundred years ago, wild animals seemed to be as plentiful as weeds.
   Because of these killings, more than a hundred types of animals have become extinct since 1800. An animal is extinct when there are no more animals of that type.
   One type of extinct animal is the passenger pigeon. At one time, these birds were so plentiful that flocks of them used to blacken the sky. Now the passenger pigeon is gone forever. Think of that. You will never get to see a living passenger pigeon or any of the other animals that have become extinct. The only place you can see those animals is in a museum, where they are stuffed and mounted.
1. Are house cats extinct?

• What's the answer? (Response: *No*.)

2. Is that question answered by **words** or a **deduction**?

• What's the answer? (Response: *Deduction*.)
• That's right, the passage does not contain this sentence: "House cats are not extinct." You figure out the answer by making a deduction.
• Here's the deduction: **Animals are extinct when there are no more animals of that type. There are still many house cats. Therefore, house cats are not extinct.**

3. Name one type of extinct animal.

• What's the answer? (Response: *The passenger pigeon*.)

4. **Words** or **deduction**?

• Is the question answered by **words** or by a **deduction**? (Response: *Words*.)

Lesson 57 **273**

- Read the sentence that contains words that answer the question. (Response: *One type of extinct animal is the passenger pigeon.*)

5. How many types of animals have become extinct since 1800?

- What's the answer? (Response: *More than a hundred.*)

6. **Words** or **deduction**?

- Is the question answered by **words** or by a **deduction**? (Response: *Words.*)
- Read the sentence that contains the words that answer the question. (Response: Because of these killings, more than a hundred types of animals have become extinct since 1800.)

7. The dodo bird is extinct. How many animals of that type are alive today?

- What's the answer? (Idea: *None.*)

8. **Words** or **deduction**?

- Is the question answered by **words** or by a **deduction**? (Response: *Deduction.*)
- Here's the deduction: **Animals are extinct when there are no more animals of that type. The dodo bird is extinct. Therefore, there are no more animals of that type.**
- You'll write the answers later.

READING

EXERCISE 6
FOCUS QUESTION

1. Everybody, find part C. ✓
2. What's the focus question for today's lesson? (Response: *How did Sylvia feel about living on her foster mother's farm?*)

EXERCISE 7
READING ALOUD (OPTIONAL)

1. We're going to read aloud to the diamond.
- (Call on individual students to read several sentences each.)

A White Heron
by Sarah Orne Jewett
Part 1
Focus Question: How did Sylvia feel about living on her foster mother's farm?

The woods were filled with shadows one June evening, but a bright sunset still glimmered faintly among the trunks of the trees. A girl named Sylvia was driving a cow from the pasture to her home. Sylvia had spent more than an hour looking for the cow and had finally found her hiding behind a huckleberry bush.

Sylvia and the cow were going away from the sunset and into the dark woods. But they were familiar with the path, and the darkness did not bother them.

Sylvia wondered what her foster mother, Mrs. Tilley, would say because they were so late. But Mrs. Tilley knew how difficult it was to find the cow. She had chased the beast many times herself. As she waited, she was only thankful that Sylvia could help her. Sylvia seemed to love the out-of-doors, and Mrs. Tilley thought that being outdoors was a good change for an orphan girl who had grown up in a town.

The companions followed the shady road. The cow took slow steps, and the girl took very fast ones. The cow stopped at the brook to drink, and Sylvia stood still and waited. She let her bare feet cool themselves in the water while the great twilight moths struck softly against her. She waded on through the brook as the cow moved away, and she listened to the waterbirds with pleasure.

There was a stirring in the great boughs overhead. They were full of little birds that seemed to be wide awake and going about their business. Sylvia began to feel sleepy as she walked along. However, it was not much farther to the house, and the air was soft and sweet.

She was not often in the woods so late as this. The darkness made her feel as if she were a part of the gray shadows and the moving leaves. She was thinking how long it seemed since she had first come to her foster mother's farm a year ago. Sylvia wondered if everything was still going on in the noisy town just the same as when she had lived there. ♦

SILENT READING

1. Read the rest of the lesson to yourselves and be ready to answer some questions.

It seemed to Sylvia that she had never been alive at all before she came to live at her foster mother's farm. It was a beautiful place to live, and she never wished to go back to the town. The thought of the children who used to chase and frighten her made her hurry along the path to escape from the shadows of the trees.

Suddenly, she was horror-struck to hear a clear whistle not very far away. It was not a bird's whistle. It sounded more like a boy's. Sylvia stepped aside into the bushes, but she was too late. The whistler had discovered her, and he called out in a cheerful voice, "Hello, little girl, how far is it to the road?"

Trembling, Sylvia answered quietly, "A long distance."

She did not dare to look at the tall young man, who carried a gun over his shoulder. But Sylvia came out of the bushes and again followed the cow, while the young man walked alongside her.

"I have been hunting for some birds," the stranger said kindly, "and I have lost my way. Don't be afraid," he added gallantly. "Speak up and tell me what your name is and whether you think I can spend the night at your house and go out hunting early in the morning." ★

Sylvia was more alarmed than before. Would her foster mother blame her for this? She hung her head, but she managed to answer "Sylvia" when her companion again asked her name.

Mrs. Tilley was standing in the doorway when the trio came into view. The cow gave a loud moo as if to explain the situation.

Mrs. Tilley said, "Yes, you'd better speak up for yourself, you naughty old cow! Where'd she hide herself this time, Sylvia?" But Sylvia kept silent.

The young man stood his gun beside the door and dropped a heavy gamebag next to it. Then he said good evening to Mrs. Tilley. He repeated his story and asked if he could have a night's lodging.

"Put me anywhere you like," he said. "I must be off early in the morning, before day, but I am very hungry indeed. Could you give me some milk?"

"Dear sakes, yes," said Mrs. Tilley. "You might do better if you went out to the main road, but you're welcome to what we've got. I'll milk the cow right now, and you make yourself at home. Now step round and set a plate for the gentleman, Sylvia!"

Sylvia promptly stepped. She was glad to have something to do, and she was hungry herself.

- How did Sylvia feel about living on her foster mother's farm? (Ideas: *She loved being outdoors; the farm made her feel alive.*)
- Why didn't Sylvia like the town? (Ideas: *The other children made fun of her; it was noisy and crowded.*)
- Why do you think Sylvia didn't dare to look at the young man? (Ideas: *She was afraid of him; he was a stranger; she was shy.*)
- How do you think Sylvia feels about hunting? Explain your answer. (Ideas: *She probably doesn't like hunting because she loves living things; she probably doesn't like hunting because guns are noisy.*)
- What do you think will happen in the next part of the story? (Ideas: *The stranger will ask Sylvia to go hunting with him; the stranger will rob Sylvia and her foster mother.*)

PAIRED PRACTICE (OPTIONAL)

1. Now you'll read in pairs.
- Whoever read second the last time will read first today.
- Remember to start at the diamond and switch at the star.
2. (Observe students and answer questions as needed.)

AFTER READING

INDEPENDENT WORK

1. Do all the items in your workbook and textbook for this lesson.
2. (The independent work in this lesson includes the following activities.)
   - Story details
   - Vocabulary
   - Figurative language
   - Deductions
   - Character traits
   - Comparisons
   - Inference
   - Vocabulary review
   - Comprehension
   - Writing

WORKCHECK

1. (Using the Answer Key, read the questions and answers for the workbook.)
2. (Have students read their answers for the textbook activities.)
3. (Have two or three students read their writing assignments aloud. Comment on each assignment.)
4. (Have students correct and turn in their work.)

LANGUAGE ARTS GUIDE

(Students should complete the appropriate exercises in the *Language Arts Guide* after completing lesson 57. See *Language Arts Guide* for details.)

The *Language Arts Guide* is not a core component of *Reading Mastery* Classic.

57

A WORD LISTS

1
Hard Words
1. heron
2. trio
3. Sylvia
4. wilderness
5. gallant
6. pigeon

2
Word Practice
1. Circe
2. Calypso
3. Scylla

3
New Vocabulary
1. heron
2. foster parent
3. huckleberry
4. bough
5. gallant
6. trio
7. game

B VOCABULARY DEFINITIONS

1. **heron**—*Herons* are birds that wade through water and eat frogs and fish. Herons usually have tall, thin legs and a long, S-shaped neck. The picture shows a *white heron.*
   • Describe a heron.

2. **foster parent**—A *foster parent* is somebody who brings up a child but is not the child's real parent.
   • What do we call somebody who brings up a child but is not the child's real parent?

3. **huckleberry**—A *huckleberry* is a small purple or black berry that grows on bushes.
   • What is a huckleberry?

4. **bough**—A *bough* of a tree is a branch of the tree.
   • What is a branch of a tree?

5. **gallant**—Somebody who is *gallant* is brave and noble.
   • What's another way of saying *He was a noble warrior?*

6. **trio**—A *trio* is a group of three.
   • What's another way of saying *A group of three went to the river?*

7. **game**—Wild animals that are hunted are called *game.*
   • What do we call wild animals that are hunted?

C READING

A White Heron
*by Sarah Orne Jewett**
Part 1

Focus Question: How did Sylvia feel about living on her foster mother's farm?

The woods were filled with shadows one June evening, but a bright sunset still glimmered faintly among the trunks of the trees. A girl named Sylvia was driving a cow from the pasture to her home. Sylvia had spent more than an hour looking for the cow and had finally found her hiding behind a huckleberry bush.

Sylvia and the cow were going away from the sunset and into the dark woods. But they were familiar with the path, and the darkness did not bother them.

Sylvia wondered what her foster mother, Mrs. Tilley, would say because they were so late. But Mrs. Tilley knew how difficult it was to find the cow. She had chased the beast many times herself. As she waited, she was only thankful that Sylvia could help her. Sylvia seemed to love the out-of-doors, and Mrs. Tilley thought that being outdoors was a good change for an orphan girl who had grown up in a town.

The companions followed the shady road. The cow took slow steps, and the girl took very fast ones. The cow stopped at the brook to drink, and Sylvia stood still and waited. She let her bare feet cool themselves in the water while the great twilight moths struck softly against her. She waded on through the brook as the cow moved away, and she listened to the waterbirds with pleasure.

There was a stirring in the great boughs overhead. They were full of little birds that seemed to be wide awake and going about their business. Sylvia began to feel sleepy as she walked along. However, it was not much farther to the house, and the air was soft and sweet.

She was not often in the woods so late as this. The darkness made her feel as if she were a part of the gray shadows and the moving leaves. She was thinking how long it seemed since she had first come to her foster mother's farm a year ago. Sylvia wondered if everything was still going on in the noisy town just the same as when she had lived there.◆

It seemed to Sylvia that she had never been alive at all before she came to live at her foster mother's farm. It was a beautiful place to live, and she never wished to go back to the town. The thought of the children who used to chase and frighten her made her hurry along the path to escape from the shadows of the trees.

---
* *Adapted for young readers*

Suddenly, she was horror-struck to hear a clear whistle not very far away. It was not a bird's whistle. It sounded more like a boy's. Sylvia stepped aside into the bushes, but she was too late. The whistler had discovered her, and he called out in a cheerful voice, "Hello, little girl, how far is it to the road?"

Trembling, Sylvia answered quietly, "A long distance."

She did not dare to look at the tall young man, who carried a gun over his shoulder. But Sylvia came out of the bushes and again followed the cow, while the young man walked alongside her.

"I have been hunting for some birds," the stranger said kindly, "and I have lost my way. Don't be afraid," he added gallantly. "Speak up and tell me what your name is and whether you think I can spend the night at your house and go out hunting early in the morning."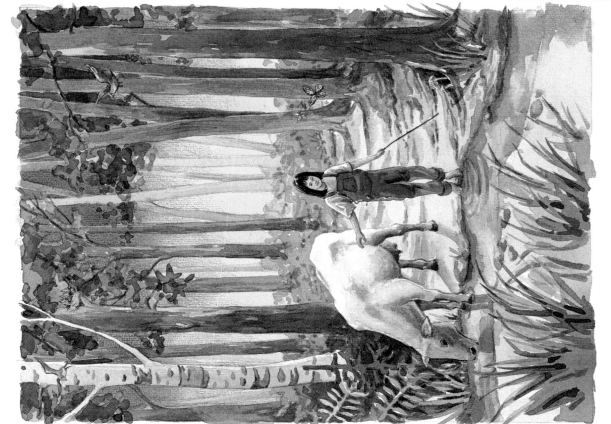

Sylvia was more alarmed than before. Would her foster mother blame her for this? She hung her head, but she managed to answer "Sylvia" when her companion again asked her name.

Mrs. Tilley was standing in the door-way when the trio came into view. The cow gave a loud moo as if to explain the situation.

Mrs. Tilley said, "Yes, you'd better speak up for yourself, you naughty old cow! Where'd she hide herself this time, Sylvia?" But Sylvia kept silent.

The young man stood his gun beside the door and dropped a heavy gamebag next to it. Then he said good evening to Mrs. Tilley. He repeated his story and asked if he could have a night's lodging.

"Put me anywhere you like," he said. "I must be off early in the morning, before day, but I am very hungry indeed. Could you give me some milk?"

"Dear sakes, yes," said Mrs. Tilley. "You might do better if you went out to the main road, but you're welcome to what we've got. I'll milk the cow right now, and you make yourself at home. Now step round and set a plate for the gentleman, Sylvia!"

Sylvia promptly stepped. She was glad to have something to do, and she was hungry herself.

D INFERENCE

Write the answers for items 1–8.

You have to answer different types of questions about the passages you read. Some questions are answered by words in the passage. Other questions are *not* answered by words in the passage. You have to figure out the answer by making a deduction.

The following passage includes both types of questions.

More about Ecology

Two hundred years ago, many people were not concerned with ecology. They believed there was no end to the different types of wildlife, so they killed wild animals by the hundreds of thousands. When we look back on these killings, we may feel shocked. But for the people who lived two hundred years ago, wild animals seemed to be as plentiful as weeds.

Because of these killings, more than a hundred types of animals have become extinct since 1800. An animal is extinct when there are no more animals of that type.

One type of extinct animal is the passenger pigeon. At one time, these birds were so plentiful that flocks of them used to blacken the sky. Now the passenger pigeon is gone forever. Think of that. You will never get to see a living passenger pigeon or any of the other animals that have become extinct. The only place you can see those animals is in a museum, where they are stuffed and mounted.

1. Are house cats extinct?
2. Is that question answered by **words** or a **deduction**?
3. Name one type of extinct animal.
4. **Words** or **deduction**?
5. How many types of animals have become extinct since 1800?
6. **Words** or **deduction**?
7. The dodo bird is extinct. How many animals of that type are alive today?
8. **Words** or **deduction**?

E DEDUCTIONS

Write the answers about the deductions.
Oliver believed that if he studied, he would pass the test. Oliver studied for the test.
1. So, what did Oliver believe would happen?

Nadia believed that if you ate an apple a day you would stay healthy. Nadia ate an apple every day.
2. So, what did Nadia believe would happen?

F VOCABULARY REVIEW

unprecedented
maneuver
devoted
spurn
endured
regard

For each item, write the correct word.
1. When you move skillfully, you ▮▮▮.
2. When you consider something, you ▮▮▮ it.
3. Something that has never occurred before is ▮▮▮.

G COMPREHENSION

Write the answers.
1. How did Sylvia feel about living on her foster mother's farm?
2. Why didn't Sylvia like the town?
3. Why do you think Sylvia didn't dare to look at the young man?
4. How do you think Sylvia feels about hunting? Explain your answer.
5. What do you think will happen in the next part of the story?

H WRITING

Where would you rather live, on a farm or in a town?

Write an essay that explains your answer. Try to answer the following questions:

- What are the advantages of living on a farm?
- What are the disadvantages of living on a farm?
- What are the advantages of living in a town?
- What are the disadvantages of living in a town?
- Where would you rather live? Why?

Make your essay at least sixty words long.

Name _____

A STORY DETAILS

Write or circle the answers.

1. Sylvia was ___ who lived on a farm.
   • a vacationer • a farmhand • an orphan

2. Where had Sylvia lived before coming to the farm?

3. Sylvia thought she had never been ___ at all before coming to the farm.
   • scared • alive • punished

4. Which place did Sylvia enjoy more, the town or the farm?

5. How had the children in town treated Sylvia?

6. What was the young man doing in the woods?

7. Was Sylvia bold or shy?

8. What was the name of the person who owned the farm?

9. That person was Sylvia's ___.
   • employer • mother • foster parent

57

B VOCABULARY

Write the correct words in the blanks.

regarded	suitable
appealed	humiliating
unprecedented	maneuvered

1. The starving boy _____ to the sympathy of the crowd.

2. They _____ the criminal as a dangerous person.

3. He _____ the shopping cart past the fallen cans.

4. The pitcher made an _____ number of strikeouts.

C FIGURATIVE LANGUAGE

For each statement, write **simile**, **metaphor**, or **exaggeration**.

1. Her face was like a pale star.

2. The apartment was a prison.

3. The day was like a dream.

D DEDUCTIONS

Complete each deduction.

Every element has an atomic weight. Argon is an element.

1. What's the conclusion about argon?

_____

_____

Horses eat grass. A palomino is a horse.

2. What's the conclusion about a palomino?

_____

_____

E CHARACTER TRAITS

Write whether each phrase describes **Sylvia**, **Mrs. Tilley**, or **the stranger.**

1. Very shy

2. Whistled loudly

3. An orphan

4. Owned a farm

5. Felt like a part of the woods

6. Hunted for animals

F COMPARISONS

Write **Odyssey** if the event occurred in *The Odyssey.* Write **Yarn** if the event occurred in "Mystery Yarn."

1. Telemachus was one of the suitors.

2. Telemachus helped defeat the suitors.

3. The suitors took a test that involved unwinding string.

4. The suitors took a test that involved a bow and arrow.

▬ GO TO PART D IN YOUR TEXTBOOK. ▬